Reporting Test Disabilities and English-Language Learners

Summary of a Workshop

Judith Anderson Koenig, editor

Board on Testing and Assessment
Center for Education
Division of Behavioral and Social Sciences and Education

NATIONAL ACADEMY PRESS
Washington, DC

NOTICE: The project that is the subject of this report was approved by the Governing Board of the National Research Council, whose members are drawn from the councils of the National Academy of Sciences, the National Academy of Engineering, and the Institute of Medicine. The members of the committee responsible for the report were chosen for their special competences and with regard for appropriate balance.

This study was supported by Contract/Grant No. R215U990016 between the National Academy of Sciences and the United States Department of Education. Any opinions, findings, conclusions, or recommendations expressed in this report are those of the author and do not necessarily reflect the views of the organizations or agencies that provided support for the project.

International Standard Book Number 0-309-08472-5

Additional copies of this report are available from

National Academy Press
2101 Constitution Avenue, NW
Box 285
Washington, DC 20055
800/624-6242
202/334-3313 (in the Washington Metropolitan Area)
<http://www.nap.edu>

Suggested citation:

National Research Council. (2002). *Reporting Test Results for Students with Disabilities and English-Language Learners, Summary of a Workshop.* Judith Anderson Koenig, editor. Board on Testing and Assessment, Center for Education, Division of Behavioral and Social Sciences and Education. Washington, DC: National Academy Press.

THE NATIONAL ACADEMIES

National Academy of Sciences
National Academy of Engineering
Institute of Medicine
National Research Council

The **National Academy of Sciences** is a private, nonprofit, self-perpetuating society of distinguished scholars engaged in scientific and engineering research, dedicated to the furtherance of science and technology and to their use for the general welfare. Upon the authority of the charter granted to it by the Congress in 1863, the Academy has a mandate that requires it to advise the federal government on scientific and technical matters. Dr. Bruce M. Alberts is president of the National Academy of Sciences.

The **National Academy of Engineering** was established in 1964, under the charter of the National Academy of Sciences, as a parallel organization of outstanding engineers. It is autonomous in its administration and in the selection of its members, sharing with the National Academy of Sciences the responsibility for advising the federal government. The National Academy of Engineering also sponsors engineering programs aimed at meeting national needs, encourages education and research, and recognizes the superior achievements of engineers. Dr. Wm. A. Wulf is president of the National Academy of Engineering.

The **Institute of Medicine** was established in 1970 by the National Academy of Sciences to secure the services of eminent members of appropriate professions in the examination of policy matters pertaining to the health of the public. The Institute acts under the responsibility given to the National Academy of Sciences by its congressional charter to be an adviser to the federal government and, upon its own initiative, to identify issues of medical care, research, and education. Dr. Harvey V. Fineberg is president of the Institute of Medicine.

The **National Research Council** was organized by the National Academy of Sciences in 1916 to associate the broad community of science and technology with the Academy's purposes of furthering knowledge and advising the federal government. Functioning in accordance with general policies determined by the Academy, the Council has become the principal operating agency of both the National Academy of Sciences and the National Academy of Engineering in providing services to the government, the public, and the scientific and engineering communities. The Council is administered jointly by both Academies and the Institute of Medicine. Dr. Bruce M. Alberts and Dr. Wm. A. Wulf are chairman and vice chairman, respectively, of the National Research Council.

Acknowledgments

At the request of the U.S. Department of Education, the National Research Council's (NRC) Board on Testing and Assessment (BOTA) convened a workshop on reporting test results for individuals who receive accommodations during large-scale assessments. The workshop brought together representatives from state assessment offices, individuals familiar with testing students with disabilities and English-language learners, and measurement experts to discuss the policy, measurement, and score use considerations associated with testing students with special needs. BOTA is grateful to the many individuals whose efforts made this workshop summary possible.

The workshop was conceived by a steering committee consisting of the chair, Lauress Wise, and members Lorraine McDonnell, Margaret McLaughlin, and Charlene Rivera. This summary was executed by Judith Koenig, staff study director, to reflect a factual summary of what occurred at the workshop. We wish to thank the many workshop speakers, whose remarks stimulated a rich and wide-ranging discussion (see Appendix A for the workshop agenda). Steering committee members, as well as workshop participants, contributed questions and insights that significantly enhanced the dialogue.

We also wish to thank staff from the National Center for Education Statistics (NCES), under the direction of Gary Phillips, acting commissioner, and staff from the National Assessment Governing Board (NAGB), under the direction of Roy Truby, who were valuable sources of information for the workshop. Peggy Carr, Patricia Dabbs, and Arnold Goldstein of NCES and James Carlson, Lawrence Feinberg, and Ray Fields of NAGB provided the planning committee with important background information and were key participants in workshop discussions.

Special thanks are due to a number of individuals at the National Research Council who provided guidance and assistance at many times during the organization of the workshop and the preparation of this report. Pasquale DeVito, director of BOTA, provided expert guidance and leadership of this project. We are indebted to Patricia Morison, associate director of the Center for Education, for her advice during the planning stages of this workshop and for her review of numerous drafts of this summary. We thank Susan Hunt for her editorial assistance on this report. Special thanks go to Andrew Tompkins and Lisa Alston for their management of the operational aspects of the workshop and production of this report. We thank Kaeli Knowles for her reviews of this summary and her never-ending moral support. We are especially grateful to Kirsten Sampson Snyder and Eugenia Grohman for their deft guidance of this report through the review and production process.

This report has been reviewed in draft form by individuals chosen for their diverse perspectives and technical expertise, in accordance with procedures approved by the National Research Council's Report Review Committee. The purpose of this independent review is to provide candid and critical comments that will assist the institution in making its published report as sound as possible and to ensure that the report meets institutional standards for objectivity, evidence, and responsiveness to the study charge. The review comments and draft manuscript remain confidential to protect the integrity of the deliberative process.

We wish to thank the following individuals for their review of this report:

Diane August, consultant, Washington, DC
Lizanne DeStefano, School of Education, University of Illinois
Wayne Martin, Council of Chief State School Officers, Washington, DC
Don McLaughlin, American Institutes for Research, Palo Alto, CA
William L. Taylor, attorney at law, Washington, DC
Martha L. Thurlow, Department of Educational Psychology, University of Minnesota

Although the reviewers listed above have provided many constructive comments and suggestions, they were not asked to endorse the final draft of the report before its release. The review of this report was overseen by Marge Petit, National Center for the Improvement of Educational Assessment, Dover, NH. Appointed by the National Research Council, she was responsible for making certain that an independent examination of this report was carried out in accordance with institutional procedures and that all review comments were carefully considered. Responsibility for the final content of this report rests entirely with the author.

Contents

1

Introduction

OVERVIEW OF THE NATIONAL ASSESSMENT OF EDUCATIONAL PROGRESS

As mandated by Congress in 1969, the National Assessment of Educational Progress (NAEP) surveys the educational accomplishments of students in the United States. The assessment monitors changes in achievement, providing a measure of students' learning at critical points in their school experience (U.S. Department of Education [DoEd], 1999). Results from the assessment inform national and state policy makers about student performance, thereby playing an integral role in evaluating the conditions and progress of the nation's educational system.

NAEP includes two distinct assessment programs, referred to as "long-term trend NAEP" (or "trend NAEP") and "main NAEP," with different instrumentation, sampling, administration, and reporting practices (DoEd, 1999). Long-term trend NAEP is a collection of test items in reading, mathematics, and science that have been administered many times over the last three decades. As the name implies, long-term trend NAEP is designed to document changes in academic performance over time. It is administered to nationally representative samples of 9-, 13-, and 17-year-olds (DoEd, 1999).

Main NAEP test items reflect current thinking about what students know and can do in the NAEP subject areas. They are based on recently developed content and skill outlines in reading, writing, mathematics, science, U.S. history, world history, geography, civics, the arts, and foreign languages. Main NAEP assessments use the latest advances in assessment methodology. Typically, two subjects are tested at each biennial administration. Main NAEP results are also used to track short-term changes in performance. Main NAEP has two components: national NAEP and state NAEP.

National NAEP tests nationally representative samples of students in grades four, eight, and twelve. In most subjects, NAEP is administered two, three, or four times during a 12-year period. State NAEP assessments are administered to representative samples of students in states that elect to participate. State NAEP uses the same large-scale assessment materials as national NAEP. It is administered to grades four and eight in reading, writing, mathematics, and science (although not always in both grades in each of these subjects).

NAEP differs fundamentally from many other testing programs in that its objective is to obtain accurate measures of academic achievement for groups of students rather than for individuals. To achieve this goal NAEP uses innovative sampling, scaling, and analytic procedures. NAEP's current practice is to use a scale of 0 to 500 to summarize performance on the assessments. NAEP reports scores on this scale in a given subject area for the nation as a whole, for individual states, and for population subsets based on demographic and background characteristics. Results are tabulated over time to provide both long-term and short-term trend information. In addition to scale scores, NAEP uses achievement levels to summarize performance. The percentage of students at or above each achievement level is reported. The National Assessment Governing Board (NAGB) has established, by policy, definitions for three levels of student achievement: basic, proficient, and advanced (DoEd, 1999). The achievement levels describe the range of performance NAGB believes should be demonstrated at each grade.

Uses for NAEP Results

NAEP is intended to serve as a monitor of educational progress of students in the United States. Although NAEP results receive a fair amount of public attention, they have typically not been used for high-stakes purposes, such as for making decisions about placement, promotion, or retention. Surveys and other analyses reveal that NAEP results are used for the following purposes (National Research Council [NRC], 1999, p. 27).

1. to describe the status of the educational system,
2. to describe student performance by demographic group,
3. to identify the knowledge and skills over which students have (or do not have) mastery,
4. to support judgments about the adequacy of observed performance,
5. to argue the success or failure of instructional content and strategies,
6. to discuss relationships between achievement and school and family variables,
7. to reinforce the call for high academic standards and educational reform, and
8. to argue for system and school accountability.

The ways NAEP results are used are likely to change, however, as a result of the legislation that, at the time of this workshop, was still pending in Congress (and has since been enacted into law). At the workshop, Thomas Toch, guest scholar at the Brookings Institute, described the proposed legislation. This legislation calls for annual testing of third through eighth graders in mathematics and reading, with test results used to determine rewards or corrective actions for schools, school districts, and states. The education plan contains an adequate yearly progress element, which in effect requires that schools, school districts, and states set standards and report annual progress for students in four groups: racial/ethnic minorities, economically disadvantaged students, English-language learners, and students with disabilities. If students in each of those four groups do not make sufficient progress each year toward the state's standards, the schools, school districts, and states would be subject to corrective action. The ultimate objective is for 100 percent of the students in each of these four groups to achieve state standards for proficiency within 12 years. Schools that accomplish this goal would be eligible for financial rewards. Corrective actions for schools that do not show progress include the following: their students may be allowed to attend different public schools; the state may take over school operations; and/or the schools may be subject to other forms of restructuring.

At the time of the workshop, the proposed legislation called for comparisons to be made between state assessment results and an external test in order to encourage states to establish high standards and use high-quality tests. The Senate version of the bill, which was the one that passed, called for NAEP to fill this benchmarking role. The language was modified in the final version of the legislation, and it does not actually call for such benchmarking. The law does, however, mandate state participation in biennial NAEP assessments of fourth and eighth grade reading and mathematics, and it is expected that NAEP will serve as a benchmark for state assessments (Taylor, 2002). It was within this context—a general expectation that the proposed legislation would be adopted and that such comparisons would be required—that the workshop took place.

Including and Accommodating Students with Special Needs

Accommodations are provided to test takers with special needs in order to remove disability-related barriers to performance. The goal is to provide accommodations that compensate for a student's specific disability but do not alter the attributes measured by the assessment or give an unfair advantage to the accommodated student. Accommodations are intended to correct for the disability so that scores from an accommodated assessment measure the same attributes as scores from an assessment administered without accommodations to individuals without disabilities (NRC, 1997; Shepard, Taylor, and Betebenner, 1998; Koretz and Hamilton, 2000). However, there are no hard and fast rules for what constitutes an appropriate accommodation for a given student's special needs. Hence, there is always a risk that the accommodation over- or under-corrects in a way that distorts performance.

In 1996, NAEP began piloting testing procedures for including and accommodating students with special needs in the assessment. At the same time, a research plan was implemented to investigate the impact of the policy changes on the participation of special needs students in NAEP and to examine the effects on performance of testing with accommodations. Research has continued with subsequent assessments, and inclusion and accommodation policies are now a permanent aspect of the program.

Currently, NAEP's stewards[1] are addressing issues related to reporting the results from accommodated administrations. Beginning in 2002, NAEP will report aggregated data that combine results for those who receive accommodations and those who take the test under standard procedures. Since accommodations were not allowed prior to 1996, there is

---

[1]NAEP's stewards include National Assessment Governing Board members and staff as well as National Center for Education Statistics staff members.

some concern about the comparability of pre-1996 data to future data. That is, what effects will the new policies have on the interpretation of trends (long term as well as those based on main NAEP)?

Considerable research has been conducted on the effects of accommodations on performance on tests other than NAEP. One objective for the workshop was to learn more about the findings from the research and to consider the extent to which they generalize to NAEP. Of particular interest was research on the comparability of scores from accommodated and nonaccommodated administrations and the extent to which they can be considered to measure similar constructs.

In addition, through their efforts to comply with existing legislation (such as the Americans with Disabilities Act, the Individuals with Disabilities Education Act, and Title I), states have accumulated a good deal of experience with including and accommodating students with special needs and reporting their results. Another objective for the workshop was to learn about states' experiences in enacting their reporting policies. NAEP's stewards believed that such information would be useful as they formulate reporting policies for NAEP. Of particular interest were questions such as: What data do states include in their reports? Under what conditions are results for accommodated and nonaccommodated test takers aggregated for reporting? For what categories of students do states report disaggregated results? What, if any, complications have arisen in connection with preparing aggregated or disaggregated data? And what have been the effects of inclusion and accommodation on trend data reported for the state assessment? The fact that the new legislation is expected to require comparisons between state assessment and NAEP results makes these reporting issues are especially relevant.

OVERVIEW OF WORKSHOP

Officials with the National Center for Education Statistics asked the NRC's Board on Testing and Assessment (BOTA) to convene a workshop to assist them with their decision making about reporting results for accommodated test takers. BOTA is well positioned to assist with these questions since it has already conducted two evaluations of NAEP programs (NRC, 1999, 2001) and two studies on testing students with special needs (NRC, 1997, 2000).

The workshop brought together representatives from state assessment offices, individuals familiar with testing students with disabilities and En-

glish-language learners, and measurement experts to discuss the policy and
technical considerations associated with testing students with special needs.
The daylong workshop included four panels that explored the following
issues:

• What inclusion and accommodation policies are in effect in state
testing programs?
• What data do states report for excluded students, included and accommodated students, and students tested under standard testing conditions? How are data aggregated and disaggregated for reporting purposes?
How do states report trend data for accommodated students and for those
tested under standard testing conditions?
• What issues have states encountered as they make decisions about
reporting results for accommodated test takers?
• What does the research suggest about the effects of accommodations on test performance for English-language learners and students with
disabilities?
• What does the research suggest about the validity of scores from
accommodated administrations?
• What does the research suggest about the comparability of scores
from standard and accommodated administrations?

The first panel of workshop speakers laid out the policy and legal context for including and accommodating students with special needs in large-
scale testing. Arthur Coleman, with Nixon Peabody LLP, and Thomas
Toch, guest scholar with the Brookings Institute, addressed these issues. In
addition, Peggy Carr, associate commissioner of education at the National
Center for Education Statistics, and Jim Carlson, assistant director for psychometrics at the National Assessment Governing Board (NAGB), provided background information on NAEP's policies.

The second panel addressed state policies on accommodations and reporting results for students with disabilities and English-language learners.
Speakers included Martha Thurlow, director of the National Center on
Educational Outcomes at the University of Minnesota, and Laura Golden
and Lynne Sacks, researchers at George Washington University's Center for
Equity and Excellence in Education (CEEE), who highlighted findings
from their surveys of states' policies. In addition, representatives from two
state offices of assessment—Scott Trimble (Kentucky) and Phyllis Stolp
(Texas)—spoke about the policies of their respective states.

Panel three consisted of researchers who have investigated the effects of accommodations on test performance. John Mazzeo, executive director of the Educational Testing Service's School and College Services, spoke about research conducted on NAEP. Other speakers included Stephen Elliott, professor at the University of Wisconsin; Gerald Tindal, professor at the University of Oregon; Jamal Abedi, adjunct professor at the UCLA Graduate School of Education and director of technical projects at the National Center for Research on Evaluation, Standards, and Student Testing (CRESST); and Laura Hamilton, behavioral scientist with the RAND Corporation.

The final panel consisted of four discussants who were asked to summarize and synthesize the ideas presented during the workshop and to highlight issues in need of further exploration and research. Panel speakers included Eugene Johnson, chief psychometrician at the American Institutes for Research; David Malouf, educational research analyst at DoEd's Office of Special Education Programs; Richard Durán, professor at the University of California at Santa Barbara; and Margaret Goertz, co-director of the Consortium for Policy Research in Education.

OVERVIEW OF THIS REPORT

Chapter 2 provides background information on NAEP's policies for including and accommodating students with special needs and gives an overview of the research plan first implemented with the 1996 assessment. Chapter 3 summarizes information provided by Arthur Coleman on federal requirements for including and accommodating students with disabilities and English-language learners in large-scale assessment. Chapter 4 presents the findings from surveys of states' policies for including, accommodating, and reporting results for students with special needs. First-hand accounts of policies and experiences with reporting results for accommodated test takers in Texas and Kentucky appear in Chapter 5. Chapter 6 highlights the main points made by the speakers in the fourth panel, who discussed findings from research on the effects of accommodations on NAEP and on other tests. Chapter 7 concludes the report with a summary of discussants' remarks.

2

Background and Problem Statement

Peggy Carr, associate commissioner for assessment at the National Center for Education Statistics, and Jim Carlson, assistant director for psychometrics at the National Assessment Governing Board (NAGB), made the opening presentations, providing historical context about the inclusion of students with special needs in NAEP and laying out what they hoped to learn from the days' interactions. Carlson began by describing a series of resolutions through which NAGB established a plan for conducting research on the effects of including students with disabilities and English-language learners in the assessment. In these resolutions, the Board articulated dual priorities of including students who can "meaningfully take part" in the assessment while also maintaining the integrity of the trend data that are considered a key component of NAEP. According to Peggy Carr, the resolution and research plan provided "a bridge to the future" in which NAEP would be more inclusive, and "a bridge to the past" in which NAEP would continue to provide meaningful trend information. One of the chief concerns was that new policies and procedures would not interfere with the ability to report trends in the important subjects both for the nation and for the states.

In her presentation, Carr described the research plan implemented with the 1996 mathematics assessment. This plan called for data to be collected for three samples, referred to as S1, S2, and S3. The S1 sample maintained the status quo, in which administration procedures were handled in the same way as in the early 1990s. In the early 1990s, a student with an individual education plan (IEP) could be excluded from the assessment if he or she was mainstreamed less than 50 percent of the time in academic subjects or was judged to be incapable of participating meaningfully in the assessment (U.S. DoEd, 1994). Any students identified by school officials as "limited English proficient" could be excluded if he or she was "a native speaker of language other than English," had been enrolled "in an English-speaking school for less than two years," and was "judged to be incapable of taking part in the assessment" (U.S. DoEd, 1994: pg. 126).

In the S2 sample, revisions were made to the criteria given to schools for determining whether to include students with special needs, but no accommodations or adaptations were offered. For S2, students with IEPs were to be included unless

> the school's IEP team determined that the student could not participate; or the student's cognitive functioning was so severely impaired that she or he could not participate; or the student's IEP required that the student be tested with an accommodation or adaptation, and that the student could not demonstrate his or her knowledge without that accommodation (Mazzeo, Carlson, Voelkl, and Lutkus, 2000: pg. 10).

Students designated as limited English proficient by school officials and

> receiving academic instruction in English for three years or more were to be included in the assessment. [Those] receiving instruction in English for less than three years were to be included unless school staff judged them to be incapable of participating in the assessment in English (Mazzeo, Carlson, Voelkl, and Lutkus, 2000: pg. 10).

In S3, the revised inclusion criteria were used, and accommodations were made available for students with disabilities and English-language learners. These students were allowed to take the test with the accommodations that they routinely received in their state or district assessments, as long as the accommodations were approved for use on NAEP. NAEP-approved accommodations for the 1996 administrations included extended time; individual or small group administration; a large-print version of the test; transcription, oral reading, or signing of directions; and use of bilingual dictionaries in mathematics. Final decisions about which accommodations to provide to students in S3 were made by school authorities. The criteria for the three samples are summarized in Box 2-1.

Analyses of the 1996 data revealed no differences in participation rates between the S1 and S2 samples. Thus, the S1 criteria were discontinued, and research was based on samples of schools that applied either the S2 or

---

BOX 2-1
Inclusion and Accommodation Criteria Utilized in
NAEP Research Samples

S1: Students with special needs who required accommodations were not included in the assessment.
S2: Students with special needs were included, but no accommodations were provided.
S3: Students with special needs were included and accommodations were provided.

---

the S3 criteria. The research continued with the 1998 national and state NAEP reading assessment and the 2000 assessments (mathematics and science at the national level in grades four, eight, and twelve and at the state level in grades four and eight; reading at the national level in grade four). The accommodations permitted were similar to those allowed in 1996, and a bilingual booklet was offered in mathematics at grades four and eight. Reading aloud passages or questions on the reading assessment was explicitly prohibited. Alternative language versions and bilingual glossaries were not permitted on the reading or science assessments. Findings from studies in 1996, 1998, and 2000 are described in detail in Chapter 6.

Based on the research findings and other considerations, NAGB passed the following resolution in 2001 (NAGB, 2001: pg. 43):

> For the 2002 NAEP, the entire NAEP sample, for both national and state-level assessments, will be selected and treated according to the procedures followed in the S3 samples of 1998 and 2000. All students identified by their school staff as students with disabilities (SD) or limited-English proficient (LEP) and needing accommodations will be permitted to use the accommodations they receive under their usual classroom testing procedures, except those accommodations deemed to alter the construct being tested. (The most prominent of these is reading the reading assessment items aloud, or offering linguistic adaptations of the reading items, such as translations.) No oversampling of SD or LEP students is planned. In reading, trends will compare data from 2002 to the S3 sample for 1998. . . The S2 sample, in which all students were tested under standard conditions only, will be discontinued.

Through this policy NAGB adopted the criteria applied in the S3 sample as the official procedures (i.e., permitted accommodations will be provided to students who need them).

There are a number of unanswered questions about the comparability of scores from standard and nonstandard (accommodated) administrations and the effects of changes in inclusion policies on NAEP's trend information. Although an accommodation is intended to correct for the disability, there is a risk that the accommodation over- or undercorrects in a way that further distorts a student's performance and undermines validity. Thus, it cannot simply be assumed that scores from standard and nonstandard administrations are comparable. Adopting the procedures used for the S3 sample represents a significant change in NAEP's inclusion policy, since special needs students who required accommodations were not included in the pre-1996 assessments. The change in inclusion policy could mean that results from the pre-1996 assessments are not comparable to results based on the inclusion policy used for S3 (National Institute of Statistical Sciences, 2000).

One of NAEP's chief objectives is to provide information about trends in U.S. students' educational achievement, but changes in policy regarding who participates in NAEP and how the test is administered can have an impact on the comparability of trend data. Carlson and Carr both emphasized that they hoped that the day's discussions would provide them with a better understanding of the effects of accommodations on test performance and assist them as they work with others to formulate and refine NAEP's reporting policies.

3
Legal and Political Contexts for Including Students with Special Needs in Assessment Programs

Workshop speakers, Thomas Toch, guest scholar with the Brookings Institute, and Arthur Coleman, legal counsel with Nixon Peabody LLP, made presentations to lay out the political and legal context in which inclusion and accommodation occurs. Toch spoke about the proposed school reform measures that were being debated in Congress at the time of the workshop and have since passed. This legislation was described in Chapter 1, and relevant points are repeated here. Coleman spoke about the federal laws that have implications for inclusion and accommodation.

POLITICAL CONTEXT

Coleman opened his presentation by saying that there is one issue that has bipartisan agreement in Washington these days—that tests are good. Testing was a significant component of the Goals 2000: Educate America Act of 1994, the school reform measures enacted by the Clinton administration, and the Improving America's Schools Act[1] (IASA), the 1994 reauthorization of the Elementary and Secondary Education Act (ESEA). Testing is also the centerpiece of the No Child Left Behind Act, the 2001 reauthorization of the ESEA. This emphasis on testing stems from the belief that the only way to know how well students are achieving is to

---

[1] P.L. 103-328.

evaluate their performance and measure their progress. Thus, although some may regard tests as "the enemy," tests are considered a benefit in the context of federal policy because they provide a means for holding schools accountable for student progress. School systems cannot deny such a benefit to a student without a compelling reason.

The No Child Left Behind Act[2] requires states to provide for the participation of all students in their systems of assessments. The legislation requires annual testing in reading and mathematics in grades three through eight beginning with the 2005-06 school year, and testing in science at three grade levels (3-5, 6-9, and 10-12) beginning with 2007-08 [Sec 1111 (b) (3)]. With respect to students with disabilities, the legislation requires that states provide reasonable accommodations as defined under the Individuals with Disabilities Education Act (IDEA). For English-language learners, the law requires students to be assessed to the extent feasible in the language that best reflects what they know and can do. Students who have attended school in the United States for three years must receive assessments in English of their skills in reading and language arts [Sec. 1111 (b) (3) (c) (ix and x)]. Moreover, the law requires local education agencies to assess the oral language, reading, and writing skills of "limited-English proficient" students by the 2002-03 school year [Sec. 1111 (b) (7)]. The legislation also explicitly requires schools, school districts, and states to set standards and report annual progress for English-language learners and students with disabilities [Sec. (c) (VII)]. Rewards and corrective actions for schools are based on students in these groups making adequate yearly progress.

LEGAL CONTEXT

In laying out the legal context for inclusion and accommodation, Coleman noted that there is a "complex maze" of federal laws that relate to standards-based educational reform. He distinguished between laws that deal with fundamental student rights and those that are related to a particular federal grant program. Accordingly, students who are in public or private schools that are recipients of federal funds are protected by guarantees that are related to appropriate test use provisions. Such laws include

---

[2] Some of the details about the No Child Left Behind Act are based on Toch's presentation, and some are drawn from a paper by William Taylor (2002) describing the terms of the adopted legislation.

the Fourteenth Amendment, Title VI of the Civil Rights Act of 1964, the Equal Educational Opportunities Act, Section 504 of the 1973 Rehabilitation Act, and Title II of the Americans with Disabilities Act (ADA) of 1990.

The Fourteenth Amendment to the Constitution guarantees protection from discrimination and provides for due process. Public schools are prohibited from denying students the equal protection of the law or life, liberty, or property interests without due process. Title VI of the Civil Rights Act of 1964 prohibits discrimination on the basis of race, color, or national origin and, according to Coleman, has been interpreted as requiring inclusion of English-language learners in testing. This interpretation is based on the premise that testing is a benefit; categorically excluding a student from testing amounts to denying him or her a benefit and potentially severely limiting future educational opportunities. The Equal Educational Opportunities Act protects the rights of language-minority students. The ADA and Section 504 protect the rights of individuals with disabilities.

Federal grant programs, on the other hand, have very specific requirements that do not trigger student rights of action in court, but instead condition the award and use of federal funds around certain specified test use practices. Laws that fall into this category are Titles I and VII of the 1994 ESEA, the Goals 2000: Educate America Act, and the No Child Left Behind Act. Title I of the 1994 ESEA serves disadvantaged, high-poverty students, while Title VII serves language minority students. As noted above, Goals 2000 and No Child Left Behind promote standards-based reform efforts.

The Individuals with Disabilities Education Act (IDEA)[3] falls into the category of a grants program because it provides funds to states to serve students with disabilities, but it is also a civil rights law that extends the constitutional right of equality of educational opportunity to students with disabilities who need special education. In 1997 the IDEA was amended to better ensure that students with disabilities fully participate in public education and receive the special services detailed in their individual education plans (IEPs). The new IDEA regulations require states to include students with disabilities in statewide testing, to offer appropriate accom-

---

[3]P.L. 105-12.

modations whenever possible so that students can be included or to develop and implement alternate assessment systems to facilitate inclusion of those with the most severe disablities, and to report in a similar fashion the performance of all students. Accordingly, school districts must provide students with disabilities with a free appropriate education, which includes an IEP that is in most cases linked to the district's high standards curriculum and is provided in the least restrictive environment possible.

According to Coleman, school districts have an "affirmative obligation" to provide English-language learners with equal access to educational programs so that these students have the opportunity to become proficient in English and to achieve the high academic standards of their educational programs. School districts must ensure that their curricular and instructional programs for English-language learners are recognized as educationally sound or otherwise vouched for as legitimate educational strategies and that they are implemented effectively and monitored over time (and altered, as needed) to ensure success.

INCLUSION

Inclusion is explicitly addressed in numerous pieces of legislation. For students with disabilities, inclusion is addressed in the IDEA, Title II of the ADA, and Title I of the 1994 ESEA. The IDEA and Title I both contain specific language requiring students with disabilities to be included in statewide assessments [Sec. 612 (a) (17)] [Sec. 1111 (b) (3) (F)]. Exclusion from assessments based on disability violates Section 504 of the Rehabilitation Act [29 U.S.C. 794] and Title II of the ADA [42 U.S.C. 12132].

For English-language learners, inclusion is addressed in Title I of the 1994 ESEA and Title VI of the Civil Rights Act. Title I specifies that states must provide for the inclusion of limited-English-proficient students in Title I assessments [Sec. 1111 (b) (3) (F)]. Title VI states that to the extent that testing opportunities represent benefits or are related to educational opportunities, English-language learners must be included.

ACCOMMODATIONS

There are also legal provisions that mandate accommodations for students with special needs. Title II of the ADA specifies that students with disabilities must be provided with "appropriate accommodations where necessary" [20 U.S.C. 15412 (a) (17) (A)]. Title I of the 1994 ESEA also specifies that assessments "shall . . . provide for . . . the reasonable adaptations and accommodations for students with diverse learning needs [Sec. 1111 (b) (3) (F) (ii)] and be consistent with relevant . . . professional and technical standards [Sec.1111 (b) (3)].

Accommodations for English-language learners are addressed in Title VI of the Civil Rights Act and Title I of the ESEA. Title VI states that English-language learners must be provided appropriate accommodations (see Title VI). Title I states that English-language learners shall be assessed to the extent practicable in the language and form most likely to yield accurate and reliable information . . . in subjects other than English [Sec. 1111 (b) (3)]. Materials to assess English-language learners must measure the extent to which the student has a disability and needs special education rather than measuring his or her English skills [34 CFR part 300 532 (a) (2)].

According to Coleman, under federal law there are clearly described obligations regarding the role of the IEP team in determining how students with disabilities are included and accommodated in assessments. Furthermore, there is a clearly defined statement from the Department of Education regarding the state's obligation. That is, the state's role is to develop policies to ensure that appropriate accommodations are used, but the state cannot limit the authority of the IEP team to select suitable and appropriate accommodations.

English-language learners, on the other hand, do not have IEPs. Thus, there is no common basis for decision making about inclusion and accommodation for these students.

REPORTING

Titles I and VII of the 1994 ESEA require states to report disaggregated achievement test results for students with disabilities and English-language learners in order to monitor their progress. This requirement for reporting is continued and raised to a new status with the No Child Left Behind Act. As mentioned previously, states will be required not just to report results for students with disabilities and English-language learners, but to ensure that students in these groups make progress.

ALTERNATIVE ASSESSMENTS

For students with disabilities, there is an additional legal requirement to provide alternate assessments when appropriate accommodations cannot be provided on statewide or large-scale assessments [20 U.S.C. 1412 (a) (17) (A)]. Coleman suggested that there is no comparable provision for English-language learners because it is assumed that a language deficit is temporary and over time will be corrected. For students with disabilities there is no expectation that the disabilities will "go away."

COURT CHALLENGES

In Coleman's opinion, the most critical issue for a testing program is a clear articulation of the purposes and objectives for testing. States have a legal obligation to provide *appropriate* accommodations, but the meaning of "appropriate" varies according to the objectives for testing and the constructs being measured. Thus, when testing programs must justify decisions about accommodations, it is crucial to know what is being tested and why the accommodation is or is not appropriate. Coleman advised testing programs to make sure that their policies and practices are appropriate, in accord with federal law, and aligned with sound educational practices.

Coleman described two recent cases that dealt with the appropriateness of the accommodations for the constructs being tested and the objectives for the assessment program. In a recent case in Indiana (*Rene v. Reed*), the decision of the state appellate court was that IEP accommodations need not be provided if they would affect the validity of test results. In another case, the state of Oregon was sued by students with disabilities. State officials agreed to a settlement in which the state assumes the burden of proof for demonstrating the inappropriateness of an accommodation. This decision means that students with disabilities who have accommodations specified in their IEPs would receive those accommodations on statewide assessments unless the state of Oregon could prove the accommodations would invalidate the construct being measured. In both cases, the court made its decision after considering the overall intent of the assessment program.

Coleman stressed that one factor behind many lawsuits is the extent to which high stakes are tied to the assessment. He finds that federal law—to the extent that it provides a foundation for a private damages claim in court—is generally not going to be triggered unless a student is denied an opportunity or a benefit. This can result when a student has not received the accommodations he or she requested and then fails a test that has high stakes attached to the results, such as placement, promotion, or graduation decisions. In addition, Coleman knows of several cases in which students did not claim that they were denied a promotion or graduation opportunity but that they were stigmatized or traumatized by the testing experience.

Coleman speculated that changes could be on the horizon as a result of the recent education legislation. To date, litigation has primarily been associated with tests that have high stakes for students, such as placement, promotion, and graduation tests. Coleman foresees that new sorts of cases could arise when the current legislation is implemented. He referred to these as second-generation claims in which students are impacted by the accountability measures enacted for schools and/or school districts, such as corrective actions imposed as a result of a school's poor test performance. To date, there has been no litigation associated with NAEP because it has not been used to provide instructional benefits or opportunities to individual students. However, NAEP may have a new role in the new legislation because comparisons may be made between NAEP results and states' assessment results. Coleman speculated that NAEP may be drawn into such second-generation claims if high-stakes decisions were based on such comparisons.

4

State Policies on Including, Accommodating, and Reporting Results for Students with Special Needs

As stated earlier, one objective for the workshop was to learn more about states' policies for reporting results of accommodated tests. Given the mandates of recent legislation, states have accumulated a good deal of experience with including and accommodating students with special needs and reporting their results. NAEP's stewards were interested in hearing about states' policies and the lessons learned during the policy development process. The goal was to learn about findings from research and surveys as well as to hear firsthand accounts of states' experiences. This information is useful for NAEP's stewards as they formulate new policy for NAEP and is especially relevant, given the comparisons between NAEP and state assessment results expected to be required by law.

This chapter summarizes remarks made by the second panel of workshop speakers. This panel included three researchers who have conducted surveys of states' reporting policies and two representatives from state assessment programs. Martha Thurlow, director of the National Center on Educational Outcomes at the University of Minnesota, reported on findings from her research on states' policies and practices for including and accommodating students with disabilities in statewide assessments and reporting their scores. Researchers with George Washington University's Center for Equity and Excellence in Education (CEEE) have conducted similar studies on states' policies for English-language learners. One study, designed to collect information on policies for 2000-2001, is currently under way. Another study, examining policies for 1998-1999, has been published

19

(Rivera, Stansfield, Scialdone, and Sharkey, 2000). Lynne Sacks and Laura Golden, researchers with the CEEE, gave an overview of findings from the earlier study and highlighted preliminary findings from the study currently under way. This chapter summarizes major findings from the surveys and adds comments from the personal experiences of the two state assessment directors, Scott Trimble, director of assessment for Kentucky, and Phyllis Stolp, director of development and administration, student assessment programs for Texas. Trimble's and Stolp's comments about the policies and experiences in their respective states are described in further detail in Chapter 5. The chapter concludes with discussion about the complications involved in interpreting results that include scores for accommodated test takers.

INCLUSION AND ACCOMMODATION POLICIES

As background, the speakers first discussed their research findings regarding states' inclusion and accommodation policies. Martha Thurlow discussed states' policies for including and accommodating students with disabilities; Lynne Sacks and Laura Golden provided similar information about states' policies for English-language learners.

Policies for Students with Disabilities

According to Thurlow, all states now have a policy that articulates guidelines for including and accommodating students with disabilities. These policies typically acknowledge the idea that some changes in administration practices are acceptable because they do not alter the construct tested, while others are unacceptable because they change the construct being assessed. Thurlow noted that the majority of states (n = 39) make a distinction between acceptable and unacceptable accommodations, but they use a variety of terminology to do so (e.g., accommodation vs. modification, allowed vs. not allowed, standard vs. nonstandard, permitted vs. nonpermitted, and reportable vs. not reportable). For students with disabilities, accommodations are determined by the IEP teams, and they can be categorized as changes in the administration setting or timing (e.g., one-on-one administration, extended time), changes in test presentation (e.g., large print, Braille, read aloud), or changes in the mode for responding to the test (e.g., dictating responses, typing instead of handwriting responses, marking answers in the test booklet).

Policies for English-Language Learners

In their presentations, Lynne Sacks and Laura Golden reported that all but one of the states have policies that articulate guidelines for including English-language learners in assessments. Forty-three states have policies for providing accommodations to English-language learners. All of these states allow English-language learners to test with accommodations, and 15 states expressly prohibit certain accommodations. This information is summarized in Figure 4-1.

Accommodations for English-language learners can be classified as lin-

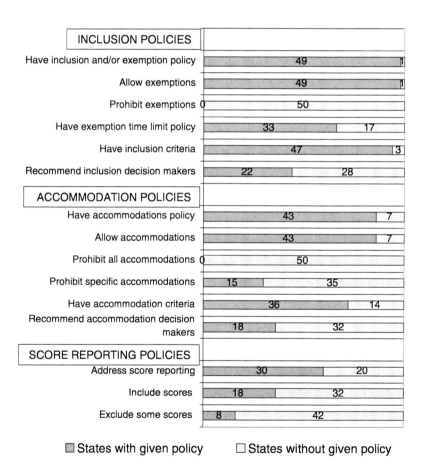

FIGURE 4-1 States' Policies for Including and Accommodating English-Language Learners in State Assessments—Preliminary Survey Findings (2000-2001).
SOURCE: Golden and Sacks (2001).

guistic or nonlinguistic. Nonlinguistic accommodations are those that have been traditionally offered to students with disabilities, such as extended time or testing in a separate room. Linguistic accommodations can be further categorized as English-language and native-language. English-language accommodations assist the student with testing in English and include adjustments such as repeating, simplifying, or clarifying test directions in English; the use of English-language glossaries; linguistic simplification of test items; and oral administration. Native-language accommodations allow the student to test in his or her native language and include use of a bilingual dictionary or a translator; oral administration in the student's native language; use of a translated version of the test; and allowing the student to respond in his or her native language. Results from the research by Sacks and Golden show that states offer more nonlinguistic than linguistic accommodations to English-language learners.

Decision making about providing accommodations for English-language learners is complicated by the fact that these students do not have IEPs, which means that there is no common basis for making these decisions. States vary with respect to who makes the decision and how it is made. The 1998-1999 survey results indicated that most often the decision was simply to let the student use whatever accommodations he or she routinely uses in the classroom situation (Rivera et al., 2000).

REPORTING POLICIES

Panel three speakers also described states' policies for reporting results for individuals who received accommodations. There are two distinct issues related to reporting such results—which students' scores are included in overall reports of test results and whether or not group-level (or disaggregated) results are reported. Each issue is taken up separately below.

Policies for Reporting Overall Results

Thurlow's findings indicate that states' policies for reporting results for students with disabilities tend to differ depending on whether students received approved or nonapproved accommodations. Nearly all states (n = 46) plan to report results for students with disabilities who use approved accommodations by aggregating those scores with scores of other test takers. However, methods and reporting policies for students using nonapproved accommodations vary considerably among states. Thurlow's findings indicated that 25 states planned to report scores of students who used nonapproved accommodations. Eleven of these states will aggregate these scores with other scores; twelve will report these scores separately from other scores; and two plan to report both ways.

A variety of policies are in effect in the remaining 25 states. In three states, students who use nonapproved accommodations will be assigned the lowest possible score or a score of zero. Six states indicated they plan to "count" (n = 3) or "not count" (n = 3) scores for examinees who use nonapproved accommodations, but these states did not explicitly indicate their policies for reporting such scores. Two states had not yet finalized their reporting policies at the time of the survey. Fourteen states have other plans for reporting scores, and many of these indicated that nonapproved accommodations were not allowed or that students who needed these accommodations would take the state's alternate assessment. These findings are displayed in Figure 4-2 and Table 4-1 and are more fully described in Thurlow (2001a).

FIGURE 4-2 States' Policies for Reporting Scores from Tests Taken with Nonapproved Accommodations (2001).
SOURCE: Thurlow (2001a).

TABLE 4-1 Responses of State Directors of Special Education to NCEO On-line Survey

State	Approved Accommodations	Nonapproved Accommodations
Alabama	No Decision	Separate
Alaska	Aggregated	Separate
Arizona	Aggregated	Separate
Arkansas	Separate	Aggregated
California	Aggregated	Counted
Colorado	Aggregated	Other
Connecticut	Aggregated	No Decision
Delaware	Aggregated	Separate
Florida	Separate	Other
Georgia	Aggregated, Separate	Aggregated, Separate, Counted
Hawaii	Aggregated	Aggregated
Idaho	Aggregated	Aggregated
Illinois	Aggregated	Aggregated
Indiana	Aggregated, Separate	Lowest Score
Iowa	Aggregated	Not Counted
Kansas	Aggregated	Separate
Kentucky	Aggregated	Other
Louisiana	Aggregated	Aggregated, Separate
Maine	Aggregated	Other
Maryland	Other	Other
Massachusetts	Aggregated	Aggregated
Michigan	Aggregated	No Decision
Minnesota	Aggregated	Other
Mississippi	Aggregated	Not Counted
Missouri	Aggregated	Aggregated
Montana	Aggregated	Separate
Nebraska	Aggregated	Aggregated
Nevada	Aggregated	Separate
New Hampshire	Aggregated	Lowest Score
New Jersey	Aggregated	Other
New Mexico	Aggregated, Separate	Other
New York	Aggregated	Aggregated
North Carolina	Aggregated	Not Counted
North Dakota	Aggregated	Aggregated
Ohio	Aggregated	Counted
Oklahoma	Aggregated, Separate	Other
Oregon	Aggregated	Separate
Pennsylvania	Aggregated	Other
Rhode Island	Aggregated	Aggregated

TABLE 4-1 Continued

State	Approved Accommodations	Nonapproved Accommodations
South Carolina	Aggregated	Separate
South Dakota	Aggregated	Separate
Tennessee	Aggregated	Other
Texas	Aggregated	Other
Utah	Aggregated	Separate
Vermont	Aggregated	Separate
Virginia	Aggregated	Aggregated
Washington	Aggregated	Counted
West Virginia	Aggregated	Other
Wisconsin	Aggregated	Other
Wyoming	Aggregated	Score Zero

Note: Data from Thompson and Thurlow (2001).

Sacks' and Golden's findings indicate that not all states have policies about reporting results of English-language learners, although the number of states with policies has increased since the 1998-1999 survey. Their most recent findings show that 30 states now have policies, as compared to only 17 for the earlier survey. Of these 30 states, 18 aggregate the scores for English-language learners with results for other test takers. The presenters commented that they did not yet have information on how reporting is handled in the other states. This information is portrayed in Figures 4-2 and 4-3.

Policies and Concerns About Reporting Group-Level Results

The federal legislation passed in January 2002 makes states accountable for the yearly progress of English-language learners and for students with disabilities, thus requiring the reporting of disaggregated results for both groups. This requirement was not in place at the time the various surveys were conducted, and few states indicated that they report disaggregated results by disability status or by limited-English-proficiency status. The topic of reporting disaggregated results provoked considerable discussion at the workshop and presenters, discussants, and participants commented about a number of issues related to group-level reporting.

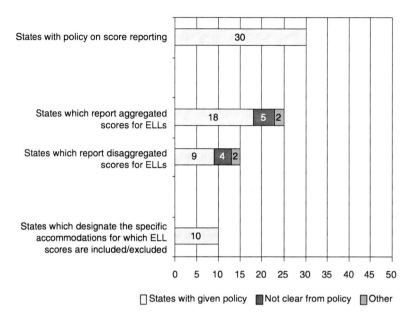

FIGURE 4-3 States' Policies for Reporting Results for English-Language Learners who Receive Accommodations on State Assessments—Preliminary Survey Findings (2000-2001).
SOURCE: Golden and Sacks (2001).

The first issue concerns the meaningfulness of disaggregated results. Eugene Johnson, chief psychometrician at the American Institutes for Research, and Jamal Abedi, professor at UCLA, pointed out that the categories of English-language learners and students with disabilities are very broad and comprise individuals with diverse characteristics. The group of English-language learners includes students who differ widely with respect to their native languages and their levels of proficiency with English. Similarly, the group of students with disabilities encompasses individuals with a wide variety of special needs, such as learning disabilities, visual impairments, and hearing impairments. With such within-group diversity, it is difficult to know what conclusions can be drawn about any reported group-level statistics.

Other issues arise because of the small sample sizes that result when data are disaggregated. These small sample sizes affect the level of confidence one can have in the results because statistics based on small sample sizes are less reliable and less stable. This is true for the summary statistics about test performance as well as for the percentages and other statistics that summarize demographic characteristics. Scott Trimble pointed out that these concerns about reporting results based on small sample sizes have led Kentucky to implement several measures. The state plans to provide estimates of standard error on newer reports and has set a minimum sample size for reporting disaggregated results.[1] Nevertheless, Trimble believes that many report users do not attend to standard error information. Johnson, who has served as consultant for numerous testing programs, added that interpreting standard error information for the lay public is so problematic that many programs simply resort to setting minimum sample sizes. According to Trimble, Kentucky does not report disaggregated data for any group that has 10 or fewer students. He added that while 10 seems to be a small number on which to base important decisions about a particular group of students, setting a higher minimum number would mean that a good deal of data could not be reported.

Another concern is the stability of group composition over time, an issue particularly important if the desire is to track and report valid trends for the various groupings. When the numbers are small, even slight changes in the composition of a group can produce large changes in the overall results. Such changes can occur, for instance, when geographical boundaries that make up the population of students attending a given school building are altered or when the guidelines for identifying students with special needs are refined. Hence, there may be changes in performance from one testing occasion to the next, but it is impossible to know whether they are the result of changes in the characteristics of the population or changes in the skill levels of the students.

Trimble recounted another problem that occurred in Kentucky in connection with disaggregation. For the state assessment, results are reported as achievement levels (novice, apprentice, proficient, and distinguished). It sometimes happens that all students in a particular population group score at the same level. When disaggregated results are reported for such a group, student scores are essentially disclosed, as the group's composition can be easily identified. In Kentucky, this violates the state laws that prohibit producing reports that permit the identification of individual student scores. Kentucky now has a quality control check intended to prevent this.

---

[1]Standard error information is intended to convey the level of uncertainty in reported results.

FACTORS COMPLICATING THE INTERPRETATION OF REPORTED RESULTS

Several workshop speakers described complications that can affect the interpretation of data reported for students with disabilities and English-language learners. As the survey results showed, states' accommodations policies vary considerably with respect to which types of accommodations are approved and nonapproved. Therefore, even if reports are confined to approved accommodations, the group of students actually included may differ from state to state, and the conditions of their testing may not be similar (disregarding for the moment the fact that the assessments also differ from state to state).

For example, consider the various ways accommodations might be provided and scores reported for students with a reading disability and Hispanic English-language learners taking a reading test. In state A, reported results could include scores for the general population testing under standard conditions, Hispanic English-language learners who took a translated Spanish version, and students with reading disabilities who received an oral administration. In state B, the oral administration and Spanish translation accommodations might be provided but considered nonapproved. Thus, unlike state A, overall score reports might not include results for these two accommodated groups. In state C, Hispanic English-language learners and students with reading disabilities may have received other types of approved accommodations (such as an English glossary for the English-language learners and extended time for the students with disabilities). Hence, like state A, their results might be included in the reports, but the scores were obtained under different conditions than in state A, conditions likely to affect performance and, consequently, the reported statistics. This variability in which accommodations are provided and which scores are included in reports complicates any attempt to make comparisons across states or between state results and NAEP (in addition to the problems posed by making comparisons of results based on different tests). This is true for reports of both aggregated and disaggregated results.

Another complication arises from states' policies regarding accommodating students with temporary disabilities. Some states approve accommodations for students who have a short-term disabling condition (e.g., a broken arm) that incapacitates them from taking the test under standard conditions. Thus, group-level reports of results for those who received accommodations may include scores for some general education students with temporary disabilities.

A third complication arises in connection with how students are identified as having a disability or as English-language learners. As Richard Durán, professor at the University of California, Santa Barbara, pointed out, determinations about which students qualify as students with disabilities or as English-language learners are not made on the basis of empirically measurable, scientifically sound criteria. For students with disabilities, particularly those with learning disabilities or attention deficit disorder, the determination is often made only when they perform poorly in school. Similarly, a wide variety of methods are used for identifying students as English-language learners.

Durán is especially concerned about identification of English-language learners. He has found that the typical practice is to classify students as English-language learners if their proficiency in English is limited for the purposes of classroom learning. However, some states use a test to make the classification while others use the numbers of years of exposure to instruction in an English-speaking environment or other factors. Durán believes that determination of English-language learner status should be based on measured proficiency in English. He has found that it is not often done this way, in part because there are few tests of English proficiency and considerable disagreement about the quality of existing tests. This stems from the fact that there is no single theory on how to measure language proficiency. Tests vary across states as do the regulations about the number of years students are required to be in school before they must receive instruction only in English (e.g., in California the requirement is one year, but this varies across states).

The result of these inconsistencies is that the categories (i.e., English-language learner and students with disabilities) consist of heterogeneous populations. Some workshop participants thought that this problem could be overcome for students with disabilities by further refining the categories for reporting purposes, that is, categorizing by the nature of the disability or the type of accommodation provided. However, this would result in even smaller numbers of students in each category, and it would not resolve the problem of heterogeneous categories for English-language learners. These problems become more immediate with the newly implemented accountability measures that require disaggregated reporting of results for English-language learners and students with disabilities.

5

Policies and Experiences in Two States

As stated earlier, one objective for the workshop was to hear firsthand accounts about states' policies and experiences with providing accommodations and reporting results for accommodated test takers. This chapter summarizes the presentations made by Phyllis Stolp, director of development and administration for Texas, and Scott Trimble, director of assessment for Kentucky. Stolp's discussion provides an overview of Texas' statewide assessments and accommodation and reporting policies. Trimble provided similar information about Kentucky's assessment programs and policies and also presented some of the assessment results. He focused on comparisons of performance for the general population and students with disabilities who used accommodations and those who did not.

POLICIES IN TEXAS

Phyllis Stolp began by summarizing the testing programs in place in Texas. She described three components of the state assessment program, all tied to the mandatory statewide curriculum called Texas Essential Knowledge and Skills (TEKS). The first component, Texas Assessment of Academic Skills (TAAS), is the primary statewide accountability assessment that has been in place since 1990. The test is intended for students enrolled in grades three through eight and includes an exit-level component. The state requires satisfactory performance on the TAAS exit-level tests for high school graduation. TAAS assesses students in reading, writing, mathematics, science, and social studies. A Spanish version of TAAS is available for students in grades three through six.

The second component of the assessment program, which has been in place since 2000, is called the Reading Proficiency Tests in English (RPTE). These tests are designed to be used with English-language learners to monitor their progress in learning to read and understand English. The tests contain reading selections and test questions divided into three levels of reading proficiency levels (beginning, intermediate, and advanced). English-language learners in grades three through twelve are required to take the RPTE until they achieve the advanced-level rating.

The State-Developed Alternative Assessment (SDAA), designed for special education students in grades three through eight, is the third component of the assessment system. Comprising tests in reading, writing, and mathematics, the SDAA is intended for students with disabilities who receive instruction in the state curriculum but for whom TAAS is an inappropriate measure of their academic progress, even when allowable accommodations are provided. The baseline year for the SDAA was 2000.

Stolp next described Texas' accommodation policies. Accommodation decisions are made on an individual basis, and they take into consideration the student's individual needs and the modifications students routinely receive in classroom instruction. Accommodations are available to all students in Texas, including general education students. For students receiving special education services, all accommodations must be documented in the student's IEP. Accommodations must also be documented for the students served under Section 504 of the Rehabilitation Act of 1973. General education students can receive accommodations as provided to them in the classroom; for these students documentation is not required. The "bottom line" criterion, however, is that the accommodation should not cause test results to be invalid.

Stolp noted that allowable and nonallowable accommodations differ for the various assessment programs. For TAAS, allowable accommodations include oral administration in mathematics, social studies, and science; large-print and Braille test booklets; individual administration; dictating or typewriting responses to the writing test; recording answers on the test booklet; and orally responding to test items. Nonallowable accommodations include reading assistance on the writing and reading tests, use of a calculator or slide rule, use of English-language or foreign-language reference materials, and translation of test items. Additional information and lists of allowable accommodations for the RPTE and SDAA are available on the state's webpage (http://www.tea.state.tx.us/student.assessment).

The state has additional requirements and maintains records for three types of accommodations—oral administration, large print, and Braille. The state has strict criteria regarding which students may use oral administration. Oral administration is offered only for the mathematics, social studies, and sciences tests, not for reading and writing, and is available only to students who receive special education services or who have a Section 504 plan. The state also collects additional information when large-print test booklets and Braille versions are used. Large print is available for all of the state's tests. Braille is available for TAAS and for most of the SDAA.

Stolp indicated that statewide, regional, district, and student test results are reported for each assessment program for each administration. Results for students using allowable accommodations are aggregated with the test results for all students. Results are disaggregated by language status (limited English proficient versus non-English proficient) and by special education status.

POLICIES IN KENTUCKY

Trimble provided the historical context for Kentucky's inclusion and accommodation practices. Although the Kentucky Educational Reform Act (KERA) was passed in 1990, the state's policies for including students with disabilities in assessment programs had been in place for some time. From 1978 through 1990, students with disabilities could be tested and accommodated in whatever way was needed; they could be excluded from testing or tested off level (take a form of the assessment intended for an earlier grade level). However, the state's policy was to exclude results for students with disabilities in reported data. In part this policy stemmed from the fact that before 1990 the purpose for testing was primarily to monitor instruction. After 1990 and with the passage of KERA, the purpose of testing was expanded to acknowledge its role in "shaping" instruction. Furthermore, state policy makers realized that accountability systems (and public reporting of assessment data) have an effect on instruction only for those who are included in the system (and the public reports), and they implemented inclusive assessment and accountability policies to ensure that the benefits of education reform were extended to all of Kentucky's students.

Trimble said that, based on current data, the percentage of Kentucky's population of elementary and middle school children considered to have a disability is between 12 and 13 percent. This figure has changed over time and was about 8 percent in 1993. Trimble commented that it is impossible to know if there really are more students with disabilities in the state or if the increased efforts to identify and serve children with disabilities have resulted in more students with disabilities being identified.

Trimble provided some examples of the types of data reported for Kentucky's various tests. For the statewide assessment, Kentucky Instructional Results Information System (KIRIS), the reports summarize performance for the total group of test takers; they then separate the total group into students without disabilities (the "general population") and students with disabilities. The results for students with disabilities are further disaggregated for those who received accommodations and those who did not. Performance is summarized with bands that display the range of scores one standard deviation below the mean to one standard deviation above the mean. These results are compiled over time to portray performance trends for KIRIS. Trimble presented results for the fourth grade reading and science assessments, and an example appears in Figure 5-1.

In fourth grade reading, students with disabilities tended to score lower than the general population in all years but two (1995 and 1996); in those two years students with and without disabilities performed similarly. In addition, nonaccommodated students tended to perform less well than accommodated students except in 1997 and 1998 when the two groups performed similarly.

In fourth grade science, students who took the test without accommodations scored lower than the general population in all years except 1995 when they scored similarly. As with reading, nonaccommodated students tended to perform less well than students who received accommodations. In 1995, accommodated students with disabilities actually slightly outscored the general population.

Trimble discussed results for another of Kentucky's statewide assessment programs, the Kentucky Core Content Test (KCCT). He showed examples of KCCT reports for three years (1999-2001) for fourth grade reading and science. These reports summarized performance with the same sorts of bands used for KIRIS results. Results are reported for a variety of population groups including gender, racial/ethnic, limited English, and students with disabilities. As with the KIRIS data, this latter category is further disaggregated into those who used accommodations and those who

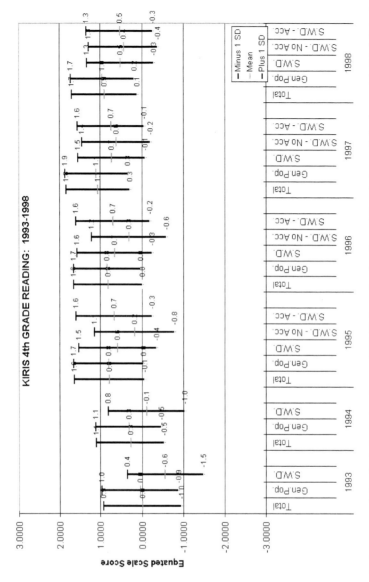

FIGURE 5-1 Kentucky Instructional Results Information System (KIRIS) Data for the General Population and Students with Disabilities in Fourth Grade Reading 1993-1998.

SOURCE: Trimble (2001).

did not. A sample report for the 2001 reading assessment appears in Figure 5-2.

Results for both subject areas and all three years showed that fourth graders with disabilities who used accommodations performed similarly to fourth graders with disabilities who took the test without accommodations, although there was more variability in the latter group. Regardless of the conditions for administration, students with disabilities did not perform as well as those without disabilities.

Trimble presented tables for the same three-year period (1999-2001) for the KCCT reading test in grades four, seven, and ten and the KCCT science test in grades four, seven, and eleven. These reports contrasted means for the total population with means for four groups (general population, students with disabilities, students with disabilities who received accommodations, and students with disabilities who did not receive accommodations). A sample of one of these tables for fourth grade reading appears in Figure 5-3.

Over the three-year period, the students with disabilities who received accommodations outperformed their nonaccommodated counterparts by 3 to 5 points in fourth grade reading. In seventh grade reading, the non-accommodated students slightly outscored the accommodated students by 3 to 6 points over the three-year period. For tenth grade reading, the non-accommodated students also outperformed the accommodated students, and the differences were quite a bit larger (from 10 to 15 points) over the three years.

Similar patterns were evident in science over the three-year period. Fourth graders with disabilities who received accommodations scored 3 to 5 points higher than those who did not receive accommodations. In seventh grade, nonaccommodated test takers scored higher than accommodated test takers by 4 to 6 points; and in eleventh grade, the difference was 11 to 13 points over the three years.

Finally, Trimble compared results for accommodated and nonaccommodated test takers on the KCCT with similar data from the Comprehensive Test of Basic Skills (CTBS) and NAEP, noting that these are the sorts of comparisons that may soon be required by law. On the CTBS, students with disabilities in Kentucky who took the test without accommodations attained overall mean scores that were higher than for those who received accommodations. This finding was consistent across the grade levels (third, sixth, and ninth). On NAEP's mathematics and science assessments in 2000, mean scaled scores were identical for Kentucky's fourth graders with

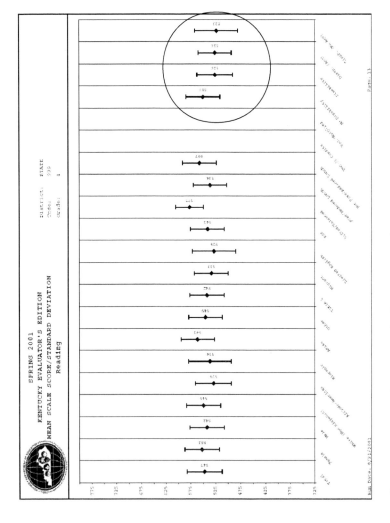

FIGURE 5-2 Kentucky Core Content Reading Test Results for Various Population Groups in Spring 2001.
SOURCE: Trimble (2001).

KCCT Reading: Grade 4

Grade 4	READING					
	1999		2000		2001	
All	544.0		546.0		547.0	
N-Count	48,251	100.0%	49,225	100.0%	49,578	100.0%
General Population	547		548		550	
N-Count	42,366	87.8%	43,533	88.4%	43,747	88.2%
(DIFFERENCE)	3.0		2.0		3.0	
Students with Disabilities	523		523		526	
N-Count	5,885	12.2%	5,692	11.6%	5,831	11.8%
(DIFFERENCE)	-21.0		-23.0		-21.0	
Accommodated	524		524		526	
N-Count	4,818	10.0%	4,463	9.1%	4,582	9.2%
(DIFFERENCE)	-20.0		-22.0		-21.0	
Nonaccommodated	519		521		523	
N-Count	1,067	2.2%	1,229	2.5%	1,249	2.5%
(DIFFERENCE)	-25.0		-25.0		-24.0	

FIGURE 5-3 Differences in Mean Performance Between the General Population and Students with Disabilities on Kentucky's Core Content Test (KCCT) in Grade 4 Reading.

disabilities who received accommodations on NAEP and those who did not receive accommodations. On the other hand, the means in mathematics and science for Kentucky's eighth graders with disabilities who were not accommodated on NAEP were slightly higher (by 2 scale score points) than for those who were accommodated. Trimble concluded that these results show that performance on the KCCT and NAEP appears to be reasonably consistent.

6

Effects of Accommodations on
Test Performance

One objective of the workshop was to consider the extent to which scores for accommodated examinees are valid for their intended uses and comparable to scores for nonaccommodated examinees. This is a critical issue in the interpretation of results for accommodated test takers and results that include scores from accommodated and standard administrations. To accomplish this objective, researchers who have investigated the effects of accommodations on test performance were asked to discuss their findings. This chapter summarizes their presentations. The first presentation focused on investigations with NAEP. The remainder of the studies dealt with other tests, several of which included released NAEP items.

RESEARCH ON NAEP

John Mazzeo, executive director of the Educational Testing Service's School and College Services, described research conducted on the NAEP administrations in 1996, 1998, and 2000. He noted that there were multiple purposes for the research: (1) to document the effects of the inclusion and accommodation policies on participation rates for students with special needs; (2) to examine the effects of accommodations on performance results; (3) to evaluate the effects of increased participation on the measurement of trends; and (4) to examine the impact of inclusion and accommodation on the technical quality of the results.

The multi-sample design implemented in 1996 permitted three sorts of comparisons. Comparisons of results from the S1 (original inclusion criteria, no accommodations) and S2 (new inclusion criteria, no accommodations) samples allowed study of the effects of changing the inclusion criteria. Comparisons of the S2 and S3 (new inclusion criteria, accommodations allowed) samples allowed study of the effects of providing accommodations. Comparisons of the S1 and S3 samples allowed examination of the net effect of making both types of changes.

Participation Rates for the
1996 Mathematics and Science Assessments

Mazzeo highlighted some of the major findings on participation rates based on the 1996 mathematics and science assessments of fourth and eighth graders. For students with disabilities, comparisons of S1 and S2 revealed that simply changing inclusion criteria, without offering accommodations, had little impact on rates of participation. On the other hand, comparisons of S1 and S3 showed that providing accommodations did increase the number of students who participated in the assessment at grades four and eight.

For English-language learners, comparisons of S1 and S2 suggested that the revised criteria resulted in less participation at grade four, when accommodations were not offered. Comparisons of S1 and S3 showed that offering accommodations in conjunction with the revised inclusion criteria increased participation rates in both grades. Offering accommodations (which included a Spanish language version of the mathematics assessment) had the biggest impact on English-language learners who needed to be tested in Spanish.

Several of the overall findings appear below:

• 42 to 44 percent of the students with disabilities were regularly tested by their schools with accommodations, and 19 to 37 percent were tested with accommodations in NAEP.

• 22 to 36 percent of English-language learners were regularly tested by their schools with accommodations, and 6 to 30 percent were tested with accommodations in NAEP.

• Some students with disabilities and English-language learners who did not regularly receive accommodations were given them in NAEP, but not all of those who regularly received accommodations were given accommodations in NAEP.

• Some students with disabilities were included in the assessment even though their IEPs suggested that they should have been excluded from testing.

Effects of Accommodations on Technical Characteristics of the Items

The remaining research questions required examination of test score and item-level performance. Use of the multi-sample design meant that estimation of the NAEP scale score distributions could be conducted separately for the three samples. One of the research questions was whether the results from standard and nonstandard administrations could be "fit" with the same item response theory (IRT) model.[1] Two kinds of analyses were used to answer this question: differential item functioning (DIF) analyses and comparisons of IRT model fit. DIF analyses involved comparing performances of accommodated and standard test takers on each administered item, looking for differences in the way the groups performed on the item when ability level is held constant.[2] Comparisons of IRT model fit were handled by examining item fit indices estimated in the S2 sample (no accommodations) and the S3 sample (accommodations allowed). Differences were found for some items.

To provide a context for judgments about the results, the incidence of DIF for standard and accommodated test takers was compared to the incidence of DIF for African-American and white examinees. In fourth grade science, 37 percent of the items exhibited DIF for accommodated versus standard test takers, suggesting that these items were more difficult for accommodated examinees. When comparing African-American and white examinees, only 10 percent of the items showed evidence of DIF. DIF was

---

[1]Item response theory (IRT) is a statistical model that calculates the probability of responding a certain way (e.g., correctly) on an item as a function of underlying ability. A number of IRT models exist, each with differing assumptions. The analyses examined the extent to which patterns in the data for accommodated and nonaccommodated test takers could be explained by the same IRT model. See Lord (1980) or Hambleton, Swaminathan, and Rogers (1991) for more information on IRT. See National Research Council (1997, pp. 182-183) for a discussion of IRT in the context of testing students with disabilities.

[2]Differential item functioning is said to occur if an item is more difficult for one group than for another, when the groups are matched on their total test score (or on ability level, when IRT is used). See Holland and Wainer (1993) or Camilli and Shepard (1994) for more information on DIF.

also found in twelfth grade science where 28 percent of the items appeared to be differentially difficult for accommodated test takers. In contrast, only 12 percent of the items showed DIF in comparisons of African-American and white examinees.

For the item fit indices, the researchers developed a way to collect baseline data about how much variation in fit indices would be likely to occur "naturally." These baseline estimates were derived by randomly splitting one of the S2 samples into two equivalent half-samples. The researchers conducted the model fit analyses separately for the S1, S2, and S3 samples and also for the half-samples of the S2 sample. They used the natural variation for statistics calculated for the separate half-samples as a basis for evaluating the differences observed in comparing the other three samples. Overall the differences occurred less often in the "real" data than in the half-samples (only one incident of misfit appeared to be significant, in eighth grade science). The IRT model appeared to fit data from the S3 sample somewhat better than the S2 sample.

Effects of Accommodations on NAEP Scale Scores

Another aspect of the research was comparison of reported NAEP results under the different accommodation and inclusion conditions. Again, the researchers estimated NAEP scale score distributions separately for the S1, S2, and S3 samples as well as for the equivalent half-samples of S2. They compared average scale scores for the entire sample, various demographic groups, students with disabilities, and English-language learners as calculated in each of the samples. Comparisons of group mean scale scores as calculated in the S2 and S3 samples revealed some differences. The researchers compared the number of observed differences to the number of differences that occurred when group mean scale scores calculated for the S2 half-samples were compared. Fewer differences in group means were observed when the S2 and S3 results were compared than when the results for the S2 half-samples were compared. In science, nine differences were found for the half-samples compared to five differences in comparing statistics based on S2 with those based on S3. In mathematics, three differences were found, all at grade 12. (See Mazzeo, Carlson, Voelkl, and Lutkus, 2000, for further details about the analyses of the 1996 assessment.)

Findings from the 1998 Reading Assessment

Results from analyses of the 1996 assessment data suggested issues to investigate further in the 1998 reading assessment, which was designed to report state results as well as national results for fourth and eighth graders. As stated previously, the S1 criteria were dropped, and in each of the participating states, the sample was split into two subsamples. Roughly half of the schools were part of the S2 sample (no accommodations were permitted); the other half were part of the S3 sample (accommodations were permitted).

The researchers compared both participation rates and scale score results. Comparisons across the S2 and S3 samples revealed that in most states the participation rate was higher in S3 for students with disabilities but not for English-language learners. Mazzeo believes that this finding was not surprising given that the accommodations for English-language learners did not include a Spanish-language version, linguistic modifications of the items, or oral administration, although extended time and small group (or one-on-one) administration were allowed.

Comparisons of average scale scores for the S2 and S3 samples revealed very small differences at both grades. The researchers devised a way to examine the differences in average scale scores in combination with the change in participation rates from S2 to S3. For the fourth grade sample, this analysis revealed a negative relationship between average scores and participation rates. That is, in the vast majority of states, higher participation rates were associated with lower mean scores. In some states, the participation rate was as much as 5 percent higher for S3 than for S2, while mean scores were as much as 4 points lower for S3 than for S2. Other states had smaller changes.

Findings from the 2000 Mathematics Assessment

Analyses continued with the 2000 mathematics assessment of fourth and eighth graders. For this assessment, a design similar to that used in 1998 was implemented, but this time a Spanish bilingual booklet was offered for English-language learners who needed the accommodation. Comparisons of participation rates across the S2 and S3 samples revealed a substantial increase in inclusion. This time the increases were comparable for students with disabilities and English-language learners.

Scale scores were calculated in the S2 and S3 samples for both grades four and eight, and states were rank ordered according to their reported results for S2 and S3. Comparisons of states' rank orderings revealed few differences.

Analyses were again conducted to examine differences in average scale scores in combination with changes in participation rates. As with the 1998 assessment, a negative relationship between average scale scores and participation rates was found when results were compared for S2 and S3 for eighth graders. In some states the difference in means between S2 and S3 samples was as much as 4 to 5 points. Mazzeo speculated that this finding signifies that increased inclusion may result in lower overall scores; additional research is needed on this point.

STUDIES AT THE UNIVERSITY OF WISCONSIN

Stephen Elliott, professor at the University of Wisconsin, summarized findings from research he and his colleagues have conducted on the effects of accommodations on test performance. All four studies compared performance of students with disabilities and students without disabilities. A key characteristic of the studies was that they relied on a design in which each student took the test under both accommodated and nonaccommodated conditions, thus serving as his or her own "control." To facilitate this aspect of the research design, multiple equivalent test forms were used, and each subject took two forms of the test—one form under accommodated conditions and one under nonaccommodated conditions. The researchers used counterbalanced designs[3] in their investigations, randomizing the order of the accommodated versus nonaccommodated conditions as well as the form that was used under the two conditions.

The researchers used "effect sizes" to summarize their findings. An effect size is a ratio in which the numerator is the difference between two means (e.g., the difference between the mean for students without disabilities and the mean for students with disabilities on a given test; or the difference between the means when students take the test with accommodations

---

[3]In a counterbalanced design, one group of subjects is tested in one sequence of conditions while another group is tested in a different sequence. The subjects must be randomly assigned to the different sequences (Plutchik, 1974).

and without accommodations). The denominator of the ratio is a standard deviation, typically that of the overall population or of the "majority" or comparison group. The researchers used a commonly accepted scheme to categorize effect sizes into large (> .80), medium (.40 to .80), small (< .40), zero, and negative effects (Cohen and Cohen, 1983).

A common framework for interpreting the validity of accommodations is based on discussions by Phillips (1994) and Shepard, Taylor, and Betebenner (1998) of ways to evaluate whether scores obtained with and without accommodations have comparable meanings. As described by Shepard et al., if accommodations are working as intended, an interaction should be present between educational status (e.g., students with disabilities and students without disabilities) and accommodation conditions (e.g., accommodated and not accommodated). The accommodation should improve the average score for a group of students with disabilities, but should have little or no effect on the average score of a group of non-disabled students. If an accommodation improves the performance of both groups, providing it only to certain students (those with a specific disability) is considered to be unfair. Figure 6-1 portrays a visual depiction of the 2 × 2 experimental design used to test for this interaction effect. An interaction effect would be said to exist if the mean score for examinees in group C were higher than the mean score for group A, and the mean scores for groups B and D were similar. The interaction effect was used in Elliott's studies (and others in this chapter) as the criterion for judging the validity of scores from acommodated administration.

	Target population	General population
Not Accommodated	A	B
Accommodated	C	D

FIGURE 6-1 Tabular Depiction of Criteria for Evaluating the Validity of Scores from an Accommoded Administration[a]

[a]An interaction effect is considered to exist if the mean score in cell C is higher than the mean in cell A and the means for cells B and D are similar.
SOURCE: Malouf (2001).

Effects of Accommodation "Packages" on
Mathematics and Science Performance Assessments

The first study Elliott described focused on the effects of accommodations on mathematics and science performance assessment tasks. This research was an extension of an earlier study published in 2001 (see Elliott, Kratochwill, and McKevitt, 2001) which produced very similar findings. The participants included 218 fourth graders from urban, suburban, and rural districts, 145 without disabilities and 73 with disabilities. All students with disabilities received accommodations based on teacher recommendations and/or their IEPs. Most students with disabilities received "packages" of accommodations, rather than just a single accommodation. The most frequently used accommodations for students with disabilities participating in this study were

- Verbal encouragement of effort (60 students)
- Extra time (60 students)
- Orally read directions (60 students)
- Simplify language in directions (55 students)
- Reread subtask directions (54 students)
- Read test questions and content to student (46 students)

Students without disabilities were randomly assigned to one of three test conditions: (1) no accommodations, (2) a package of accommodations (i.e., extra time, support with understanding directions and reading words, and verbal encouragement), and (3) an individualized accommodation condition based on the IEP or teacher-recommended accommodations. The students took state-developed mathematics and science performance assessments. Teachers or research project staff administered performance tasks in four one-hour sessions over the course of several weeks.

Effect sizes were calculated by comparing students' mean performance under accommodated and nonaccommodated conditions. Comparisons of the means for the two groups under the two accommodation conditions revealed a large effect (.88) for students with disabilities. However, a medium effect (.44) was found for students without disabilities. In addition, comparisons of individual-level performance with and without accommodations revealed medium to large effect sizes (.40 or higher) for approximately 78 percent of students with disabilities and 55 percent of students without disabilities. Effect sizes were in the small or zero range for approximately 10 percent of the students with disabilities and 32 percent of the students without disabilities. Negative effects were found for about 12 percent of the students with disabilities and 13 percent of the students without disabilities (negative effects indicate that students performed better under nonaccommodated conditions than under accommodated conditions). Together, these findings indicated that the interaction effect was not present, thus raising questions about the appropriateness of the accommodations.

Effects of Accommodations on Mathematics Test Scores

The second study Elliott discussed was an experimental analysis of the effects of accommodations on performance on mathematics items (Schulte, Elliott, and Kratochwill, 2000). The participants included 86 fourth graders, half of whom had disabilities. The students were given the Terra-Nova Multiple Assessments Practice Activities mathematics assessment and the Terra-Nova Multiple Assessments mathematics subtest (composed of multiple-choice and constructed-response items). Students without disabilities were randomly paired with students with disabilities within each school, and both students in each pair received the accommodations listed on the IEP for the student with disabilities. All students participated in a practice session to become familiar with the accommodations and test procedures.

Findings from this study indicated that both groups of students benefited from the testing accommodations; thus, again, the interaction effect was not present, leading to questions about the validity of scores when accommodations were used. Small effect sizes were found for students without disabilities; effect sizes were in the small to medium range for students with disabilities. One explanation for these findings may be that constructed-response items are more challenging for all students (i.e., they involve higher levels of reading and thinking skills), and the accommodations may have removed barriers to performance for both groups.

Effects of Extra Time on Mathematics Test Scores

Elliott presented findings from a third study (Marquart and Elliott, 2000), which focused on the effects of extra time accommodations. The research was based on 69 eighth graders who took a short form of a Terra-Nova mathematics test composed entirely of multiple-choice items. One-third of the participants were students with disabilities who had extra time listed on their IEPs; one-third were students whom teachers, using a rating form developed by researchers, had identified as "at-risk"; and one-third were students functioning at or above grade-level. Students had 20 minutes to complete the test under the standard time condition and up to double that time for the extra time condition. Again, random assignment was used to determine the order of the accommodated and not-accommodated conditions and the form used under each condition. Tests were administered during mathematics class or in a study hall, and students from all three groups were included in each testing session. Participants also responded to surveys.

Findings indicated that students with disabilities and students without disabilities did not differ significantly in the amount of change between their test scores obtained under the standard and extended time conditions. Further, no statistically significant differences were found between students without disabilities and the at-risk students in the amount of change between scores under the two conditions. These findings led the researchers to conclude that the extended time accommodation did not appear to have invalidated scores on the mathematics tasks. In addition, the survey results indicated that, under the extended time conditions, the majority of students felt more comfortable and less frustrated, were more motivated, thought they performed better, thought the test seemed easier, and preferred taking the test with that accommodation.

Effects of Oral Administration on Reading Test Scores

The final study Elliott described examined the effects of using read-aloud accommodations on a Terra-Nova reading test administered to eighth graders (McKevitt and Elliott, 2001). Elliott explained that oral reading of a reading test is a frequently used example of an invalid testing accommodation, although few studies have empirically examined this assertion. Oral administration is considered a permissible accommodation on reading tests in nine states but not in Wisconsin or Iowa where the study was conducted.

Study participants consisted of 48 teachers and 79 students (40 students with disabilities and 39 without disabilities). For each student, the teacher identified appropriate accommodations from a list developed by the researchers. The teachers' selections of accommodations were based on the cognitive demands of the test, the students' IEPs, and the teachers' knowledge about their students. Participants were randomly assigned to one of two test conditions. In Condition 1, 21 students with disabilities and 20 students without disabilities completed one part of the test with no accommodations and the other part with teacher-recommended accommodations (excluding reading test content aloud if recommended). In Condition 2, 19 students with disabilities and 19 without disabilities completed one part of the test with no accommodations and the other part with read-aloud accommodations in addition to those recommended by the teacher. The part of the test completed with and without accommodations was randomly determined by flipping a coin.

Analyses revealed that students without disabilities scored statistically significantly higher than students with disabilities on all parts of the test. Effect sizes were calculated by subtracting each student's nonaccommodated test score from his or her accommodated test score, then dividing by the standard deviation of the nonaccommodated test scores for the entire sample. The average effect sizes associated with the use of teacher-recommended accommodations were small for students with disabilities (.25) and negative (–.05) for students without disabilities. Average effect sizes associated with the use of read-aloud plus teacher-recommended accommodations were small and nearly similar for the two groups, .22 for students with disabilities and .24 for those without disabilities. Additional post hoc analyses revealed considerable individual variability. Elliott noted, for example, that half of all students with disabilities and 38 percent of students without disabilities had at least a small effect associated with use of the accommodations. No statistically significant interaction effects were found between group and test condition. Elliott pointed out that this study adds evidence to support the popular view that oral reading of a reading test has an invalidating effect on the test scores.

Discussion and Synthesis of Research Findings

In summarizing the key conclusions from the four studies, Elliott noted that they all showed that accommodations affect the test scores of a majority of students with disabilities and some students without disabilities, although there was significant individual variability. He cautioned that the comparability of test scores is questionable when some students who would benefit from accommodations are allowed the accommodations and others are not.

Elliott concluded by highlighting some critical issues for researchers, policy makers, and test publishers. He urged test publishers to be clearer about the intended skills assessed by a test. He distinguished between the "target skills" that a test is intended to measure and the "access skills" that are needed to demonstrate performance on the target skills. For instance, the target skill measured by a test may be reading comprehension, while vision is an access skill needed to read the test. Thus, a visually handicapped student might need a large-print or Braille version of a test to demonstrate his or her proficiency level with respect to the target skill. Elliott believes that educators' tasks of deciding upon appropriate accommodations could be made easier if test publishers were more explicit about the target skills being tested. He also maintained that educators need more professional development about assessment and testing accommodations.

In addition, Elliott called for more experimental research using diverse samples of students and various types of items in mathematics and language arts, although he acknowledged that conducting such research is challenging. He urged states to maintain better records of the number of students accommodated and the specific accommodations used; this will make it easier to conduct research and to evaluate trends over time.

STUDIES AT THE UNIVERSITY OF OREGON

Gerald Tindal, professor at the University of Oregon, made a presentation on various studies he has conducted. He began by summarizing the results of several surveys of teachers' knowledge about accommodations and examinees' perceptions about the benefits of accommodations. One survey queried teachers about permissible accommodations in their states. The results showed that the responding teachers correctly identified allowable accommodations about half the time, and special education teachers responded correctly about as often as general education teachers. Another survey examined the extent to which teachers identified appropriate accommodations for students. Results indicated that teachers tended to recommend accommodations that did not in fact assist the test taker. Tindal's surveys also showed that examinees did not accurately identify when an accommodation helped and when it did not. Test takers almost always believed they benefited from an accommodation, but the test results did not always support this notion. Based on these survey results, Tindal concludes that (1) teachers overprescribe test alterations; (2) teachers' knowledge of appropriate accommodations may be suspect; and (3) students overrate their ability to benefit from test alterations.

Effects of Oral Administration on Mathematics Test Scores

Tindal described several experimental studies he and his colleagues have conducted. One study investigated the effects of certain presentation and response accommodations on performance on a mathematics test (Tindal, Heath, Hollenbeck, Almond, and Harniss, 1998). Under the presentation accommodation, teachers read a mathematics test aloud (rather than students reading items to themselves); under the response accommodation, students marked answers in their test booklets (rather than on an answer sheet). Study participants consisted of 481 fourth graders—403 general education students and 78 special education students. All participated in both response conditions (marking in the test booklet and filling in the bubbles on the answer sheet), with the order of participation in the conditions counterbalanced (see footnote 3). The test takers were randomly assigned to one of the presentation conditions (standard versus read-aloud). In the read-aloud presentation condition, the teacher read the entire test aloud, including instructions, problems, and item choices.

Findings indicated that general education students scored significantly higher than special education students under all conditions. General education students who received the read-aloud accommodation scored slightly higher than those who read the test themselves, although the differences were not statistically significant. However, scores for special education students who received the read-aloud accommodation were statistically significantly higher than the scores for those who did not receive this accommodation.

The researchers concluded that these findings confirmed the presence of a significant interaction effect and suggested that the read-aloud accommodation is valid for mathematics items. They noted one caveat, however: For this study the read-aloud accommodation was group administered, which Tindal believes may have introduced cuing problems. That is, most students in a class know which students perform best on tests, and, because the tests consisted of multiple-choice items, they need only watch to see when these students mark their answers.

Tindal conducted a follow-up study in which the read-aloud accommodation was provided via video and handled in small-group sessions to overcome the cuing problems. The video was used with 2,000 students in 10 states. Findings indicated statistically significant differences between the means for special education and general education students and between the means for those who received the standard presentation and those who received the video presentation. There was also a statistically significant interaction of status by format—special education students who participated in the video presentation scored three points higher, on average, than those who participated in the standard administration, while no differences were evident between the means for general education students participating in the video presentation and those receiving the standard presentation.

Effects of Language Simplification on Mathematics Test Scores

In another study, Tindal and his colleagues examined the effects of providing a simplified-language version of a mathematics test to students with learning disabilities (Tindal, Anderson, Helwig, Miller, and Glasgow, 1999). Study participants were 48 seventh graders—two groups of general education students enrolled in lower mathematics classes (16 per group) and a third group of 16 students with learning disabilities who had IEPs in reading. Two test forms were developed, one consisting of items in their original form and one with the simplified items. The simplification process involved replacing indirect sentences with direct sentences; reducing the number of words in the problem; replacing passive voice with active voice; removing noun phrases and conditional clauses; replacing complex vocabulary with simpler, shorter words; and removing extraneous information.

Analyses revealed that the simplification had almost no effect on test scores; that is, students who were low readers but did not have an identified disability and those with disabilities performed equally well in either condition. Furthermore, the researchers found that 10 of the items were more difficult in their simplified form than in their original form. Tindal pointed out that the study had several limitations. Specifically, the sample size was small and the subjects were poor readers and students with disabilities, not English-language learners. He believes that the results are not conclusive and that the use of language simplification as an accommodation for students with learning disabilities needs further study.

Comparisons of Scores on Handwritten and Word-Processed Essays

Tindal and his colleagues also studied the accommodation of allowing students to use word processors to respond to essay questions instead of handwriting responses. One study (Hollenbeck, Tindal, Stieber, and Harniss, 1999) involved 80 middle school students who, as part of Oregon's statewide assessment, were given three days to compose a handwritten response to a writing assignment. Each handwritten response was transcribed into a word-processed essay, and no changes were made to correct for errors. Both the handwritten and the word-processed versions of each essay was scored during separate scoring sessions, with each response scored on six traits.

Analyses showed that for five of the six traits, the mean scores for handwritten compositions were higher than the means for the word-processed compositions, suggesting that there were differences in the ways scorers rated essays in the two response modes. For three of the traits (Ideas and Content, Organization, and Conventions), the differences between means were statistically significant. Tindall cautioned, however, that because the study participants were predominantly general education students, the findings may not generalize to students with disabilities.

Tindal and his colleagues have also conducted factor analyses[4] to study the factor structure of word-processed and handwritten response formats (Helwig, Stieber, Tindal, Hollenbeck, Heath, and Almond, 1999). For this study, 117 eighth graders (10 of whom were special education students) handwrote compositions for the Oregon statewide assessment in February, which were transcribed to word-processed essays prior to scoring. In May the same students responded to a second writing assessment, this time preparing their responses via computer. Both sets of essays were scored on the six traits. The researchers conducted factor analyses on the sets of scores for each response format.

The factor analyses showed that when only handwritten or only word-processed papers were analyzed, a single factor was identified (all traits loaded on a single factor). When data from the two writing methods were combined, two factors emerged. One factor included the trait scores based on the word-processed response, while the other included all the trait scores based on the handwritten response. Correlations between the trait scores for the different response formats were weak, even for scores on common traits. The researchers concluded from these findings that handwritten and

---

[4]Factor analysis is a statistical procedure that seeks to summarize patterns of intercorrelations among variables. The procedure involves identifying and labeling "factors," which are sets of intercorrelated variables. See Gorsuch (1983) or Crocker and Algina (1986) for additional information on factor analysis.

word-processed compositions demonstrate different skills and are judged differently by scorers.

Automated Delivery of Accommodations

Tindal closed his presentation by demonstrating his work in developing systems for computerized delivery of accommodations. His automated system presents items and answer options visually and provides options for the materials to be read aloud and/or presented in Spanish, American Sign Language, or simplified English. Tindal's goal is to package the automated system so that the student or teacher can select the appropriate set of accommodations and alter them by type of problem. Tindal encouraged participants to access his webpage (http://brt.uoregon.edu) to learn more about his research projects.

RESEARCH ON KENTUCKY'S ASSESSMENT

Laura Hamilton, behavioral scientist with the RAND Corporation, discussed research she and Daniel Koretz have conducted on the Kentucky Instructional Results Information System (KIRIS) statewide assessment. Hamilton presented findings from a study with the state's 1997 assessment (Koretz and Hamilton, 1999), which was a follow-up to an earlier study on the 1995 assessment (Koretz, 1997; Koretz and Hamilton, 1999). The 1995 assessment consisted of tests in mathematics, reading, science, and social studies given to fourth, eighth, and eleventh graders. The 1997 assessment covered the same subject areas but shifted some of the tests to fifth and seventh graders. Results from the earlier study indicated that Kentucky had been successful with including most students with disabilities, but several issues were identified for further investigation. In particular, the 1995 study revealed questionably high rates of providing accommodations, implausibly high mean scores for groups of students with disabilities, and some indication of differential item functioning in mathematics. The study of the 1997 assessment was designed to examine the stability of the earlier findings, to extend some of the analyses, and to compare results for two types of items. The 1995 assessment consisted only of open-response items (five common items administered to all students). The 1997 assessment included multiple-choice items (16 common items) as well as open-response items (4 common items).

Inclusion and Accommodation Rates

Hamilton presented data on the percentages of students who were given certain accommodations in 1997. The majority of students with disabilities received some type of accommodation; for example, 81 percent of the fourth graders with disabilities received at least one accommodation (14 percent received one accommodation; 67 percent received more than one). The most frequent accommodations were oral presentation, paraphrasing, and dictation. Use of accommodations declined as grade level went up. By grade eight, the percentage of students with disabilities who received accommodations had declined to 69 percent and by grade eleven, to 63 percent.

Comparisons of Scores for Students with Disabilities and the General Population

Hamilton summarized the overall test results for students with disabilities. The mean data were standardized in the population of non-disabled students, a process that converts means for students with disabilities to standard deviation units above or below the mean for students without disabilities.

The results indicated that, overall, students with disabilities scored lower than students without disabilities in all subject areas, at every grade level, and for both item formats (multiple-choice and open-response). The gap between the groups ranged from .4 of a standard deviation for fourth graders on the open-response science items to 1.4 of a standard deviation for eleventh graders in both item formats for reading. The gap tended to increase as grade level increased. The results for 1997 were comparable to those for 1995 for middle school and high school grades but not for elementary school students. In 1995, fourth graders with disabilities performed nearly as well as those without disabilities, with differences ranging from .1 of a standard deviation lower in science to .4 of a standard deviation lower in mathematics. In 1997, means for fourth graders with disabilities ranged from .4 of a standard deviation lower than those without disabilities on the open-ended science item to .7 of a standard deviation lower on the science multiple-choice items.

Comparisons of Scores for Accommodated and Nonaccommodated Students

The researchers also compared group performance for students with disabilities who received accommodations and those who did not. This comparison showed mixed results—in some cases, accommodated students performed less well than students who did not receive accommodations; in a few cases, this pattern was reversed. Hamilton highlighted two noteworthy findings.

The first finding of note involved comparisons of performance patterns from 1995 to 1997 for accommodated and nonaccommodated elementary students. In 1997, elementary students with disabilities who did not receive accommodations scored .6 to .8 of a standard deviation below their counterparts without disabilities on the open response portions of the assessment, depending on the subject area. In 1995, the corresponding differences for elementary students with disabilities who did not receive accommodations were similar in size to those for 1997, that is, .6 to .7 of a standard deviation below students without disabilities. In contrast, the means of elementary students with disabilities who received accommodations ranged from .4 to .7 of a standard deviation *below* their counterparts without disabilities across the various subject areas in 1997. However, in 1995, the means for elementary students with disabilities who received accommodations ranged from .1 of a standard deviation *above* to .3 of a standard deviation below the mean for elementary students without disabilities, depending on the subject area.

The second finding of note related to differences in the way students with disabilities who received accommodations and those who did not performed on certain item types. Preliminary analyses revealed that elementary students with disabilities tended to score lower on multiple-choice items than on open-response items in all subjects except reading, and the lower scores appeared to be attributable to students with disabilities who received accommodations. On the other hand, eleventh graders with disabilities tended to score lower on the open-response questions, and these lower scores appeared to be largely attributable to eleventh graders with disabilities who did not receive accommodations.

Comparisons of the Effects of Types of Accommodations

The authors further investigated the effects of accommodations by examining performance for students grouped by type of accommodation and type of disability. Hamilton and Koretz judged that some of the means for certain categories of accommodations seemed implausible not only because they were well above the mean for the non-disabled students, but also because they were so different from the means of other students who were given different sets of accommodations. Their analyses revealed that the higher levels of performance were associated with learning disabled students' use of dictation, oral presentation, and paraphrasing accommodations. In 1995, fourth graders with learning disabilities who received dictation in combination with oral presentation and/or paraphrasing outperformed students without disabilities on the reading, science, and social studies open-response items. In contrast, in 1997 fourth graders with learning disabilities who used these specific accommodations attained means on open response items near or below the means for fourth graders without disabilities.

Hamilton and Koretz further studied the effects of certain accommodations by developing several multiple regression[5] models in which the test score was the outcome variable, and the various accommodations were used as predictors.[6] Regression models were run separately for 1995 and 1997 data and the regression coefficients compared. Findings suggested some differences in the effects of the accommodations across years. The difference of most interest to the researchers was the regression coefficient associated with the use of dictation, which was .7 in 1995 and dropped to .4 in 1997. This finding indicated that use of dictation would be expected to raise a student's test score by about .7 of a standard deviation unit in 1995 but by only .4 of a standard deviation unit in 1997. The researchers believe that this difference raises questions about how the dictation accommodation was implemented in 1995.

---

[5]Multiple regression is a statistical procedure for examining the relationships between certain predictor variables and an outcome variable. One product of multiple regression is a regression coefficient for each predictor variable. The regression coefficient indicates the change in the value of the outcome variable associated with a unit increase in the predictor variable. See Pedhazur (1997) for more information on multiple regression.

[6]In this analysis, each accommodation was coded according to whether the student used it or not (i.e., 1 = used it; 0 = did not use it). As a result, the regression coefficients indicate the difference in scores between those who used the accommodation and those who did not.

Results of Item-Level Analyses

The researchers also conducted a number of item-level analyses to discern differences in the ways students with disabilities and students without disabilities responded to the items. They found that students with disabilities, whether accommodated or not, were more likely to skip items or to receive scores of zero, especially in mathematics. Also, even though students with disabilities were allowed extra time, there appeared to be a time effect—items toward the end of the test were left unanswered more often. As part of the item-level analyses, the researchers also looked at item discrimination indices.[7] They compared item discrimination indices for students without disabilities, students with disabilities who took the test without accommodations, and students with disabilities who received accommodations. They found that discrimination indices were similar for all three groups on the open-response items but differed on the multiple-choice items. In particular, the more difficult multiple-choice items tended to be less discriminating for students with disabilities than for students without disabilities. Hamilton and Koretz judged these results to be worthy of further investigation.

The researchers also conducted analyses to examine differential item functioning (see footnote 2). These analyses involved two comparisons—one between students with disabilities who did not receive accommodations and students without disabilities; the other between students with disabilities who received accommodations and students without disabilities. The analyses revealed some evidence of DIF on the mathematics tests for students with disabilities who received accommodations (but not for those who were not accommodated). DIF tended to be larger on the multiple-choice items than on the open-response items. One possible explanation for this finding was that the DIF was related to the "verbal load" of the mathematics items. That is, mathematics items that required substantial reading and writing tended to be more positively affected by accommoda-

---

[7]Item discrimination indices indicate the extent to which an item discriminates between high- and low-performing examinees. Usually, this is based on a correlation between performance on the item and total test score. For the open-response items, point-polyserial correlations were calculated between scores on a given open-response item and total scores on the open-response portion of the test. For the multiple-choice items, point-biserial correlations were calculated between the item score and the total score on the multiple-choice portion of the test. See Crocker and Algina (1986) for more information on item discrimination indices.

tions than those that had lighter reading or writing loads. Hamilton believes that this was probably related to the nature of the accommodations that involved paraphrasing, dictation, and other ways of reducing the linguistic demands of the items.

Discussion and Synthesis of Research Findings

Hamilton concluded by pointing out some of the limitations of the two studies. Although the two studies examined the implications of implementing accommodation policies on large-scale assessments, neither utilized an experimental design. Students did not serve as their own controls and were not randomly assigned to conditions as in Tindal's and Elliott's work. Hamilton called for more such work, noting that she and her colleagues have tried to launch experimental studies but have met with resistance, mostly due to a reluctance to withhold accommodations, even in a field test.

Another limitation was that there was no criterion against which to compare the performance of the different groups. This made it impossible in most cases to judge whether scores of students who used certain accommodations were more valid than those who used other accommodations or no accommodations. The researchers did not have data on why accommodations were provided to some students in some combinations and not to others; nor were they able to observe how the accommodations were implemented in practice. The data available to them did not indicate whether an accommodation was used on both the multiple-choice and open-response tests or if there were differences in the ways accommodations were implemented for the two formats.

Hamilton noted that the sample sizes for the less common disability categories (e.g., hearing or visual disabilities) were too small to support in-depth analyses. She encouraged states to incorporate and maintain better data systems to enable more refined research and more targeted studies that would address the low-prevalence disabilities.

Hamilton also called for more interviews with teachers and test administrators' like those conducted by Tindal; such studies would provide a better understanding of how educators decide which accommodations should be used. Her analyses raised some interesting questions about verbal load and other kinds of reasoning processes. She speculated that cognitive analyses of test items with both non-disabled students and students with disabilities would aid in understanding the response processes that the test items elicit and the skills actually being measured.

RESEARCH ON ENGLISH-LANGUAGE LEARNERS

Jamal Abedi, faculty member at the UCLA Graduate School of Education and director of technical projects at UCLA's National Center for Research on Evaluation, Standards, and Student Testing (CRESST), made a presentation to summarize research findings on the effects of accommodations on test performance of English-language learners. Abedi described a series of studies he has conducted, noting that many of them were sponsored by the National Center for Education Statistics, and the reports are available at the CRESST website (http://cresst96.cse.ucla.edu).

In Abedi's opinion, there are four criteria to consider in connection with providing accommodations to English-language learners. He terms the first criterion effectiveness. That is, does the accommodation strategy reduce the performance gap between English-language learners and English-proficient students? The second criterion relates to validity. Here, questions focus on the extent to which the accommodation alters the construct being measured. Abedi noted that in studies with English-language learners, it is common to use the interaction effect Elliott described to judge the validity and comparability of scores obtained under accommodated and nonaccommodated conditions. A third criterion is differential impact. In this case, the focus is on whether the effectiveness of the accommodation varies according to students' background characteristics. A final criterion is feasibility. That is, is the accommodation feasible from logistic and cost perspectives? Abedi discussed research findings within the context of these four criteria.

Studies on Linguistic Modification

Abedi first described several studies that examined the effects of using linguistic modification as an accommodation. In one study, 946 eighth graders (53 percent English-language learners and 47 percent native or "fluent" English speakers) responded to released NAEP multiple-choice and constructed-response mathematics items under accommodated and standard conditions (Abedi, Lord, Hofstetter, and Baker, 2000). Four types of accommodations were used: a linguistically simplified English version of the test, provision of a glossary, extended time (students were given an extra

25 minutes), and glossary plus extended time. One test booklet was developed for each condition, and a comparison sample of students took the test items in their original form with no accommodations. Tests were administered to intact mathematics classes with students randomly assigned to accommodation groups. All participants responded to a background questionnaire and took a NAEP reading test. The highest group mean scores were observed under the glossary plus extended time accommodation. However, this condition resulted in higher means for native English speakers as well as English-language learners, leading to questions about the validity of scores obtained under this accommodation. Performance was lowest for English learners, when they received a glossary but the time limit was not extended—a finding that the authors speculated may have resulted from information overload. The only accommodation that appeared to be effective (i.e., narrowed the score gap between native English speakers and English-language learners) was linguistic modification.

This study also included an in-depth examination of the relationships between test performance and background variables (e.g., country of origin, language of instruction, length of television viewing, attitudes toward mathematics). Multiple regression was used to examine the effects on mathematics performance of background variables, types of accommodation, and a series of interaction effects of background variables and accommodations (e.g., language of instruction by type of accommodation, television viewing by type of accommodation). Multiple regression models were run and results were compared for models that included the interaction effects and models that did not. The analyses revealed that including the interaction effects (background by type of accommodation) resulted in statistically significant increases in the amount of variance in mathematics performance that was explained by the model. The authors highlighted this finding as evidence of differential impact—the effects associated with different forms of accommodations may vary as a function of students' background characteristics.

Abedi described another study that examined the performance of 1,174 eighth graders on linguistically simplified versions of mathematics word problems, including some released NAEP items (Abedi and Lord, 2001). In this study, 372 English-language learners and 802 native English speakers responded to 20 mathematics word problems; 10 problems were linguistically simplified and 10 were in their original form. Overall, native English speakers scored higher than English-language learners. English-language learners benefited more than native English speakers when given linguistically simplified items; however, both groups of students performed better with this accommodation, leading to some concerns about the validity of the results for students who receive linguistically simplified items.

The analyses also showed some evidence of differential impact in that students from low socioeconomic backgrounds benefited more from linguistic simplification than others, and students in low-level and average mathematics classes benefited more than those in high-level mathematics and algebra classes. This finding was true for both English-language learners and native English speakers. Among the linguistic features that appeared to cause problems for students were low-frequency vocabulary and passive-voice verb constructions.

Abedi described another study (Rivera and Stansfield, 2001) that examined the effects of modifying the complexity of science items. The authors compared fourth and sixth graders' performance on the original and modified items. Scores for proficient English speakers did not increase under the linguistic simplification condition, a finding that the authors interpreted as suggesting that linguistic simplification is not a threat to validity.

Translated Tests

Abedi discussed issues associated with providing translated versions of tests. He explained that when a translated instrument is developed, the intent is to produce an assessment in a student's native language that is the same in terms of content, questions, difficulty, and constructs as the English version of the test. Abedi finds that creating a translated version of an assessment that is comparable to an English version is difficult. There is a high risk of the two versions differing in content coverage and the constructs assessed, which raises validity concerns. Even with efforts to devise ways to equate tests (Sireci, 1997) and the development of international guidelines for test translation and adaptation (Hambleton, 1994), translated assessments are technically difficult, time-consuming, and expensive to develop (National Research Council, 1999). Additionally, some languages, such as Spanish and Chinese, have multiple dialects, which limits the appropriateness of the translated version for some student populations (Olson and Goldstein, 1997).

Abedi discussed findings from a study that compared performance on NAEP word problems in mathematics under linguistic modification and Spanish translation conditions (Abedi, Lord, and Hofstetter, 1998). Participants included 1,394 eighth graders from schools with high enrollments of Spanish speakers. Three test booklets were developed. One consisted of items in their original English form, and a second consisted of items translated into Spanish. The third booklet contained linguistically modified English items for which only linguistic structures and nontechnical vocabulary were modified. Participants also took a reading test.

Preliminary analyses showed that, overall, students scored highest on the modified English version, lower on the original English version, and lowest on the Spanish version. Examination of performance by language status revealed that native English speakers scored higher than English-language learners. In addition, modification of the language of the items contributed to improved performance on 49 percent of the items, with students generally scoring higher on items with shorter problem statements.

The authors conducted a two-factor analysis of variance, finding significant differences in mathematics performance by language status and booklet type as well as a significant interaction of status by booklet type. These results persisted even after controlling for reading proficiency. Further investigation into these findings suggested that students tended to perform best on mathematics tests that were in the same language as their mathematics instruction. That is, the Hispanic English-language learners who received their mathematics instruction in English or sheltered English scored higher on the English version of items (standard or linguistically modified) than their Spanish-speaking peers. In contrast, students who received their mathematics instruction in Spanish performed higher on the Spanish-language version of the items than on the modified or standard English form of the items.

The authors also ran a series of multiple regression analyses to examine the effects of students' background variables on mathematics and reading scores. The results indicated that certain background variables, such as length of time in the United States, overall middle school grades, and number of times the student changed schools, were predictive of performance in mathematics ($R^2 = .35$) and reading ($R^2 = .27$).

Studies on Oral Administration

Albedi briefly discussed oral administration as an accommodation for English-language learners. He cited a study by Kopriva and Lowrey (1994) that surveyed students as to their preferences regarding orally administered tests. Results indicated three conditions under which students preferred oral administration in their native language: if they were new to the United States; if they were not literate in their home language; and if they had little oral or literacy proficiency in English. Students tended to prefer oral administration in English if they had been instructed in English for a long period of time and had attained a level of conversational oral proficiency in English but were not yet literate enough to read the test on their own.

Studies on the Provision of English Dictionaries

Abedi summarized findings from several studies on providing commercially published English dictionaries, noting that the findings were somewhat mixed. In one study, English dictionaries were provided to urban middle school students in Minnesota as part of a reading test (Thurlow, 2001b). The results indicated that participants who rated their English proficiency at the intermediate level appeared to benefit from this accommodation, but those who rated themselves as poor readers did not. Results from another study (Abedi, Courtney, Mirocha, Leon, and Goldberg, 2001) with fourth and eighth graders indicated that use of a published dictionary was not effective and was administratively difficult. Abedi observed that published dictionaries differ widely, and different versions can produce different results. Some have entries in "plain language" that are more understandable for English-language learners or for poor readers. He cautioned that dictionaries raise a validity concern because the definitions may provide information that the test is measuring.

Abedi introduced the idea of a customized dictionary as an alternative to a published dictionary. As the name implies, a customized dictionary is tailored to the purposes of a particular test. Only words that appear in the test items are included, and definitions are written so as not to "give away" answers to test questions. Abedi described one study on the use of customized dictionaries (Abedi, Lord, Kim, and Miyoshi, 2000). This study of 422 eighth grade students compared performance on NAEP science items in three test formats: one booklet in original format, one booklet with an English glossary and Spanish translations in the margins, and one booklet with a customized English dictionary. English-language learners scored highest when they used the customized dictionary, and there was no impact on the performance of native English speakers. Abedi interpreted the findings as suggesting that the use of the customized dictionary was effective and did not alter the construct being measured.

Recommendations for Further Study

Abedi concluded his presentation by offering several recommendations of issues needing further study. He believes that in order to more effectively identify and classify English-language learners and interpret reports of their test results, a common definition and valid criteria for classifications are needed.

Like Elliott, Abedi also urges test designers to identify the specific language demands of their assessments so that teachers can ensure that students have the language resources to demonstrate their content-area knowledge and skills. In addition, he called for test designers to modify test questions to reduce unnecessary linguistic complexity. Because reducing the level of linguistic complexity of test questions helps to narrow the performance gap between English-language learners and native English speakers, he believes this should be a priority in the development of all large-scale assessment programs.

Abedi finds that the research demonstrates that student background variables, including language background, are strong predictors of performance. He encourages states and districts to collect and maintain records on background information, including length of time in the United States, type and amount of language spoken in the home, proficiency level in English and in the student's native language, and number of years taught in both languages.

He also believes that feasibility is an important consideration. Because of the large number of English-language learners who are (or should be) assessed, providing some forms of accommodations might create logistical problems. For example, providing dictionaries or glossaries to all English-language learners, administering assessments one-on-one, or simplifying test items may exceed the capability of a school district or state. Abedi considers it imperative to perform cost-benefit analyses and to track and evaluate accommodation costs.

Finally, Abedi recommended that the effects of accommodations on the construct being measured be monitored and evaluated closely. Ideally, accommodations will reduce the language barrier for English-language learners but have no effect on native English speakers' performance. Abedi stressed that additional research is needed to examine the effectiveness, validity, and feasibility of the accommodations for different student groups.

SUMMARY OF RESEARCH FINDINGS

To help the reader assimilate the information presented in this chapter, Tables 6-1 through 6-3 highlight the key features and findings from the studies discussed in detail by the third panel of workshop speakers. Tables 6-1 and 6-2 highlight findings for students with disabilities and English-language learners, respectively. Table 6-3 summarizes findings from research on NAEP, which focused on both groups.

TABLE 6-1 Key Features and Findings from Studies on the Effects of Accommodations on Test Performance for Students with Disabilities

Accommodations Studied	Study	Grade Level	Subject Area	Major Findings
Extra time	Marquat, 2000	8th	Math	Differences in performance under accommodated and non-accommodated conditions were not statistically significant.
Oral administration	McKevitt & Elliott, 2001	8th	Reading	Both students with disabilities and general education students benefited from the accommodation.
	Tindal, Heath, Hollenbeck, Almond, & Harniss, 1998	4th	Math	Student with disabilities showed statistically significant improvement under accommodated condition, general education students did not.
Language simplification	Tindal, Anderson, Helwig, Miller, & Glasgow, 1999	7th	Math	No effects on scores for students with a reading disability or for general education students.
Typewritten responses to essay questions	Hollenbeck, Tindal, Steiber, & Harness, 1999	Middle school	Writing	Higher scores were given to handwritten responses (even though they were transcribed to word-processed format prior to scoring).

	Helwig, Stieber, Tindal, Hollenbeck, Heath, & Almond, 1999	8th	Writing	Two factors emerged, one for each response mode, hand-written vs. word-processed.
Multiple types, as specified on students' IEPs	Elliott, 2001	4th	Math and science	Student with disabilities and general education students both benefited from the accommodations.
	Schulte, Elliott, & Kratochwill, 2000	4th	Math	Student with disabilities and general education students both benefited from the accommodations.
	Koretz, 1997, Hamilton & Koretz, 1999	4th, 8th, 11th; 5th, 7th, 11th	Math, reading, science, and social studies	Student with disabilities scored lower than general education in all areas and at all grade levels. Gap between student disabilities and general education students increased as grade level went up. Mixed results comparing means for student disabilities who received accommodations and those who did not. Strongest effects observed for dictation, oral presentation, and paraphrasing. Some evidence of DIF in math for students with disabilities who received accommodations, larger for multiple-choice items than for constructed-response items.

TABLE 6-2 Key Features and Findings from Studies on the Effects of Accommodations for English-Language Learners (ELL)

Accommodations Studied	Study	Grade Level	Subject Area	Major Findings
Linguistic simplification	Abedi & Lord, 2001	8th	Math	Both ELL and native English speakers benefited from the accommodation. Low SES and low-level math students benefited more than those in high-level math and algebra.
Linguistic simplification and Spanish translation	Abedi, Lord, & Hofstetter, 1998	8th	Math	Performance varied according to language of math instruction; students who received math instruction in English scored best on modified English version.
Linguistic simplification, glossary, and extra time	Abedi, Lord, Hofstetter, & Baker, 2000	8th	Math	Both ELLs and native English speakers benefited from glossary and extra time. Effects of accommodations varied as a function of background characteristics.
Linguistic simplification and customized dictionaries	Abedi, Lord, Kim, & Miyoshi, 2000	8th	Science	ELLs improved with accommodation; no impact on native English speakers.

TABLE 6-3 Key Features and Findings from Studies on the Effects of Accommodations on

Accommodations Studied	Study	Grade Level	Type of Test	Major Findings
Extended time; individual or small group administration; large-print, transcription, oral reading, or signing of directions; bilingual dictionaries in math; bilingual Spanish booklet in math 2000	Mazzeo, Carlson, Voelkl, & Lutkus, 2000	4th and 8th	NAEP 1996, national assessment in math and science	Some evidence that IRT model fit data better when accommodations were provided (S3)[a] than when they were not provided (S2). Some evidence of DIF for accommodated 4th and 8th graders in science. Little evidence of DIF in math. Slight evidence that changes in administrative conditions had an impact on scale scores.
	Mazzeo, 1998	4th and 8th	NAEP 1998, national and state assessment in reading	Small differences in scale scores between groups when accommodations were provided (S3) and when they were not provided (S2). Higher inclusion rates were associated with lower mean scores for 4th grade state NAEP samples.
	Mazzeo, 2000	4th and 8th	NAEP 2000, national and state assessment in math	Comparisons of state's rankings based on S2 and S3 results showed few differences. Higher inclusion rates associated with lower mean scores for 8th grade State NAEP samples.

[a]Students with special needs were included in the S2 sample but accommodations were not provided; in the S3 sample, students with special needs were included and provided with accommodations.

7
Summing Up:
Synthesis of Issues and Directions
for Future Study

The daylong workshop concluded with a panel of discussants. This panel summarized and synthesized the ideas presented by previous speakers and highlighted concerns and directions for future study. Their remarks are summarized in this chapter.

TESTING IS A BENEFIT

The discussants underscored one issue that permeated the day's discussions—if students with special needs are not included in assessments, states are, in effect, excused from being accountable for their performance. Further, if scores for accommodated examinees are not reported or included in aggregate reports, there is no incentive to care about those students' test performance. Eugene Johnson, chief psychometrician with the American Institutes for Research, reiterated Arthur Coleman's point that the attitude of the law is that testing is considered to be a benefit for the tested children. Thus, states and other testing programs are obligated to ensure that all students have access to the test or an equivalent alternative, particularly in high-stakes situations.

ADAPTING TEST DESIGN TO TEST PURPOSE

Discussants also returned to another key point made by Coleman— the importance of clearly articulating both the purpose of any given assessment and the constructs being measured. Testing programs have a responsibility to ensure that accommodations provide access to the targeted constructs while also preserving them—this requires a clear understanding of what the assessment is measuring. The quandary for testing programs is how to change the way the construct is assessed without changing the meaning of the scores. This task could be simplified somewhat if test developers were clearer about what tests are designed to measure. Stephen Elliott introduced the notion of access skills and target skills[1] and encouraged test publishers to be clearer about the target skills their tests are meant to assess.

Several of the discussants and presenters called for better test design. Johnson urged consideration of ways to construct tests from the outset to minimize the effects of and the need for accommodations. For instance, much of Jamal Abedi's work has demonstrated that language simplification and use of tailored glossaries help English-language learners as well as general education students. Perhaps test developers could use simplified language from the outset in writing items and could provide glossaries for words whose definitions do not reveal answers to test questions. Richard Durán, professor at the University of California, Santa Barbara, advised that when writing test items, test developers should keep in mind the underlying purpose of the test. If understanding text written in the passive voice is not one of the targeted skills a test is designed to measure, items should be written in the more familiar active voice. Test developers should be sensitive to vocabulary usage and avoid unfamiliar words that are not related to the construct being measured. Several discussants urged exploration of the ways technology can be used to eliminate barriers to the measurement of a target skill.

VARIABILITY IN STATES' POLICIES

Another of the discussants' observations was that while every state is including students with special needs and allowing some type of accommodations, there are wide disparities in states' policies. State policies vary with respect to what accommodations are acceptable, who should receive them, how they should be implemented, whose scores should be included in score reports, and how scores should be reported. Some states also apply differ-

---

[1]Target skills are measured by the assessment. Access skills are the skills needed to demonstrate performance on the target skills.

ent accommodation and reporting policies to different state tests, and some allow accommodations that exceed those permitted by NAEP. Furthermore, the decision about what accommodations are acceptable seems to be based largely on intuition, in part because of a slim research base. The implications of this variability are discussed below.

Variability in Policies Complicates Comparisons of Aggregated Results

Margaret Goertz, co-director of the Consortium for Policy Research in Education, stressed that standardization in policies is particularly important if policy makers want to compare student assessment results across states or between states and NAEP. Because states use different assessments and often test students at different grade levels, the only way to compare student performance across states is through the state NAEP program. However, the inferences that can be based on such comparisons are limited when states have different accommodation and inclusion policies.

At present, such comparisons carry relatively low stakes for states. However, ranking in the bottom of the group may put public pressure on policy makers and educators to change instructional practice. For example, in California, low rankings led to public pressure to replace "whole language" with phonics-based reading instruction. But states do not receive rewards or suffer sanctions if they perform above or below one another.

Goertz speculated that different types of comparisons will be required under the recently passed legislation in which NAEP is expected to be used as a benchmark for comparisons with the outcomes of state assessments. For states, such comparisons are likely to be associated with higher-stakes decisions. It is possible that two types of comparisons could be made: (1) the percentage of students scoring the equivalent of "basic" or "proficient" under state standards compared to those students scoring "basic" or "proficient" on NAEP; and (2) changes over time in the percentage of students scoring in those categories on state assessments and NAEP. In either case, differences in accommodation and reporting policies between the state program and NAEP become more important. If a state's accommodation and reporting policies are more liberal, it could include more special needs (and potentially lower-scoring) students in its assessment than NAEP. The analyses conducted by John Mazzeo and his colleagues with the 1998 and 2000 assessments demonstrated that when inclusion rates were higher, mean performance was lower. Thus, it is not clear what conclusions can be drawn about the findings from such comparisons.

Variability in Policies Complicates Comparisons of Disaggregated Results

Currently, NAEP does report disaggregated data for special needs students. However, because states are requird to report disaggregated results for their own assessments, workshop participants contemplated what might happen if NAEP were to adopt a similar reporting policy. They pointed out if comparisons are to be made between NAEP and state assessment results, the lack of alignment between the accommodations and reporting policies of NAEP and of the states will become even more critical. Students with disabilities and English-language learners are defined differently by different states. Durán questioned whether it would be reasonable to attempt to compare the performance for the two groups of students on statewide achievement tests and on NAEP. For English-language learners, in particular, Durán finds that such comparisons may be confounded by the differences in the way they are included in state assessments and in NAEP. He noted that English-language learners participating in NAEP are a heterogeneous mixture of non-English background students across states. One upshot of this heterogeneity is that the data will not be comparable across states because different student populations are involved.

Variability in Implementing Policy

Another source of variability is in the way state policies are implemented. David Malouf, educational research analyst with the Office of Special Education Programs at the Department of Education, pointed out that decision making about which students receive which accommodations is primarily the responsibility of the IEP team, which has considerable flexibility in selecting accommodations needed to enable a child with a disability to participate. Malouf finds that IEP teams are frequently not well informed about the consequences of their decisions. Based on the day's discussions, he believes that IEP team decisions are clearly suspect. This is an important consideration for NAEP because NAEP accommodations are influenced by accommodations called for in the IEP. In addition, Durán noted that it is often the case that states comply "in word" with federal policies regarding maximizing participation of English-language learners in state assessments. But the way states proceed with identifying students and administering accommodations can vary greatly and has implications for interpretation of state assessment results and NAEP results.

Changes in States' Policies Complicate Interpretation of Trends

Goertz discussed the impact of changes in policy, practice, and demographics on reported results for accommodated students and on tracking student performance over time. She described four important sources of change identified by speakers: student demographics; how students with disabilities and English-language learners are served; state assessment policy on who is tested in what areas and with what kinds of tests; and state accommodation and reporting policies. Work by Thurlow (2001a), Rivera et al. (2000), and Golden and Sacks (2001) demonstrates how states are constantly refining their assessment, accommodation, and reporting policies—generally to make them more inclusive. Thus, changes in student scores, especially if scores are disaggregated for students with disabilities and English-language learners, could reflect which students are included in the assessment or in the reporting category at any given point in time, as well as measurable changes in student achievement.

EVALUATING THE VALIDITY OF ACCOMMODATIONS

As Peggy Carr, associate commissioner for assessment at the National Center for Education Statistics, asked, do accommodations level the playing field for students who receive them or do they provide an advantage? As described in Chapter 6, this question is often evaluated by testing for the presence of the interaction effect[2] discussed earlier (see Figure 6-1). Malouf and Johnson questioned the usefulness of the interaction effect as the basis for judging the validity of scores from accommodated conditions. Johnson

---

[2]That is, the performance of students in a target population (e.g., students with disabilities) is compared with and without accommodations, and a similar comparison is made for the general student population. If the accommodation boosts the performance of the students in the target population but not that of the general population, the accommodation is regarded as valid—that is, the inference can be made that the accommodation compensates for the students' specific weakness (e.g., disability or lack of English proficiency) but does not alter the construct being measured.

expressed concern about confounding between the construct being measured and the accommodation. That is, performance on the construct may rely on skills that are not the intended focus of the assessment. Accommodations may assist examinees with these skills and thus help general education students as well as those with identified special needs. Malouf echoed this, noting that while experimental researchers are increasingly using the interaction criterion, it requires further discussion. He called for psychometricians and others with expertise in large-scale assessment to further examine the utility and integrity of the interaction concept in the context of both statewide assessments and NAEP.

Durán voiced similar concerns, urging the educational measurement field to reconsider its notion of what constitutes an "inappropriate" or "invalid" accomodation. He asked, "Can we turn fear about how an assessment accommodation might distort measurement of proficiency on the targeted construct into figuring out how accommodations help measure examinees' maximum proficiency on the construct?" Durán finds that popular views of acceptable accommodations often result from confusion about what is being measured. As an example, Durán offered psychometricians' general disapproval of extended time as an acceptable accommodation. He argued that if speed is not a target skill and extended time leads to better performance for some students, there should be no problem with lengthening the time to complete the test (aside from the possible administrative burden). If the desire is to measure "speediness" in information processing, it should have been built into the definition of the targeted construct. He maintained that the finding that additional time increases the performance of general education students, as well as those with special needs, is not an issue as long as an assessment is not intended to be speeded. He encouraged the adoption of the concept of "construct-enabling" resources, that is, permitting resources that allow for better assessment of the targeted construct.

Durán cautioned, however, that building speediness into the definition of a construct could pose additional problems. For example, he noted that it is well known in the field of cognitive studies of bilingualism that individuals perform problem-solving tasks more slowly in a second language. Cognitive cross-cultural research has shown that speediness in performing problem-solving tasks is affected by culturally based socialization processes affecting how fast problem solvers approach tasks. Thus, identifying speediness as a key aspect of a content-related construct could prove problematic.

RESEARCH NEEDS

All of the discussants noted that although much research has been conducted on the effects of specific accommodations, many questions remain unanswered. The findings from various studies contradict each other and do not assist practitioners and policy makers in determining "what works." The discussants called for more research, particularly studies that utilize the within-subject randomized design described by Elliott and Gerald Tindal, in which each student serves as his or her own control, and small-scale experiments, particularly at the state level. In addition, each called for certain types of studies, as described below.

Research Should Use Refined Categories

Malouf pointed out that in most of the research discussed at the workshop, the target population was defined on the basis of a broadly-defined category—disabled versus non-disabled, English-language learners versus native-English speakers, learning disabled versus non-learning disabled, and so on. Malouf thinks that these broad categories should be replaced by specific student characteristics—reading disabled, native Spanish speaker and so on. He believes this would help in several regards. For one, IEP teams should not base their accommodation decisions on categories of disability, but instead on individual factors. Hence, research will be more useful if it focuses on the types of characteristics that IEP teams should consider. In addition, categorical labels are very gross descriptors, and there can be substantial within-category variation that mediates the effects of an accommodation, making the effects difficult to detect.

Understanding the Meaning of Aggregated Results

Johnson contemplated the meaning of test reports that combine data for accommodated and nonaccommodated test takers, given the current state of research on the comparability of results from different administrative conditions. He noted that some states are adjusting scores for accommodations by dropping the accommodated student two grade levels. He questioned whether this was a wise procedure or if some other adjustment procedure would be warranted, noting that either way experimentation is needed to decide how to combine the accommodated and nonaccommo-dated data. Further research is needed on the comparability of the results of various accommodations to the nonaccommodated results and on the comparability of the results of various accommodations to each other. Johnson suggested that it would be valuable to match the comparisons to actual state practices for measuring average yearly progress (for example, Oregon includes English-language learners in its aggregates, South Dakota excludes them). Such analyses should involve experimenting with the effects of various reporting and exclusion strategies.

Conducting Research Through Cognitive Laboratories

Johnson and Durán encouraged use of cognitive laboratories as a means for determining whether lack of access skills impede measurement of target skills. With cognitive laboratories, students work one-on-one with an administrator and answer test questions by thinking out loud. The administrator observes and records the thought process students use in arriving at their answers. Cognitive labs would allow researchers to compare how students with various disabilities react to the questions under different accommodations and to do further study into what constituted appropriate accommodations.

Further Research on the Performance of English-Language Learners

Durán commented that better understanding of the achievement of English-language learners depends on improvements in access to appropriate assessment accommodations for these students. He called for additional work to develop ways to evaluate the English proficiency of non-native English speakers. This is a particularly urgent issue in light of the recently passed legislation. He also encouraged researchers to examine the relationships between performance of achievement tests and relevant background variables, such as length of residence in the U.S., years of exposure to instruction in English, English-language proficiency levels, the characteristics of school curriculum, availability of first- and second-language resources, and other factors that interact to create different patterns of performance on assessments.

ISSUES SPECIFIC TO NAEP

How Much Inclusion Is Enough?

Malouf raised questions about what rate of participation should be expected with NAEP. The presentations and his own examination of NAEP publications indicate that inclusion rates rarely climb much above 70 percent of the students with disabilities and are usually lower. He wondered what the basis might be for judging whether this rate of inclusion was high enough, asking "Should our expectations be based on technical limits, or should they be based on other considerations?" Malouf called for reconsideration of what it means to "take part meaningfully" in the nation's educational system, and he urged NAEP's sponsors to determine ways that all students can participate.

Pressure to Disaggregate

The discussants revisited the issue of providing disaggregated results. Goertz reminded participants that states are required to report these comparisons on their state tests. NAEP's sponsors have yet to specify their plans for using data from the national or state NAEP programs to report on the performance of students with disabilities compared to that of non-disabled students and the performance of English-language learners compared to that of native speakers. Johnson maintained that it is inevitable that there will be strong pressure on NAEP to report disaggregated results for students with disabilities and for English-language learners. Although at this time sample sizes are not large enough to allow reliable reporting at the disaggregated level, NAEP's future plans for combining state and national samples may produce large enough samples to allow for disaggregation of various groups of students with disabilities. Johnson foresees that when this happens, NAEP will not be able to withstand the pressure to report disaggregated results.

Additional Research Is Needed

Malouf also recommended that additional research be conducted on the effects of accommodations on NAEP scores. He finds that the IRT (item response theory) and DIF (differential item functioning) analyses discussed by Mazzeo are broad in focus and treat accommodations as a single factor, sometimes even combining students with disabilities and English-language learners into a single population. Malouf suggested that NAEP researchers find ways to increase sample sizes to allow study of the effects of specific accommodations and to conduct more fine-grained analyses of accommodations and NAEP.

References

Abedi, J. (2001). *Assessment and accommodation for English language learners: Issues and recommendation* (Policy Brief 4). Los Angeles: University of California, Los Angeles, Center for the Study of Evaluation/National Center for Research on Evaluation, Standards, and Student Testing.

Abedi, J., Courtney, M., Mirocha, J., Leon, S., and Goldberg, J. (2001). *Language accommodation for large-scale assessment in science*. Los Angeles: University of California, Los Angeles, National Center for Research on Evaluation, Standards, and Student Testing.

Abedi, J., Hofstetter, C., Baker, E., and Lord, C. (1998). *NAEP math performance and test accommodations: Interactions with student language background* (Draft Report). Los Angeles: University of California, Los Angeles, National Center for Research on Evaluation, Standards, and Student Testing.

Abedi, J., and Lord, C. (2001). The language factors in mathematics tests. *Applied Measurement in Education, 14*(3), 219-234.

Abedi, J., Lord, C., and Hofstetter, C. (1998). *Impact of selected background variables on students' NAEP math performance*. Los Angeles: University of California, Los Angeles, Center for the Study of Evaluation/National Center for Research on Evaluation, Standards, and Student Testing.

Abedi, J., Lord, C., Hofstetter, C., and Baker, E. (2000). Impact of accommodation strategies on English language learners' test performance. *Educational Measurement: Issues and Practice, 19*(3), 16-26.

Abedi, J., Lord, C., Kim, C., and Miyoshi, J. (2000). *The effects of accommodations on the assessment of LEP students in NAEP*. Los Angeles: University of California, Los Angeles, Center for the Study of Evaluation/National Center for Research on Evaluation, Standards, and Student Testing.

Camilli, G., and Shepard, L.A. (1994). *Methods for identifying biased test items*. Thousand Oaks, CA: SAGE Publications, Inc.

Cohen, J., and Cohen, P. (1983). *Applied multiple regression/correlation analysis for the behavioral sciences.* Hillsdale, NJ: Erlbaum.

Crocker, L.M., and Algina, J. (1986). *Introduction to classical and modern test theory.* New York: CBS College Publishing.

Elliott, S.N., Kratochwill, T.R., and McKevitt, B.C. (2001). Experimental analysis of the effects of testing accommodations on the scores of students with and without disabilities. *Journal of School Psychology, 39*(1), 3-24.

Golden, L., and Sacks, L. (2001). *An overview of states' policies for reporting the performance of English-language learners on statewide assessments.* Paper prepared for workshop on Reporting Test Results for Accommodated Examinees: Policy, Measurement, and Score Use Considerations, November 28, Washington DC.

Gorsuch, R.L. (1983). *Factor analysis.* Hillsdale, NJ: Erlbaum.

Hambleton, R. (1994). Guidelines for adapting educational and psychological tests: A progress report. *European Journal of Psychological Assessment, 10*(3), 229-244.

Hambleton, R., Swaminathan, H., and Rogers, H.J. (1991). *Fundamentals of item response theory.* Newbury Park, CA: Sage.

Helwig, R., Stieber, S., Tindal, G., Hollenbeck, K., Heath, B., and Almond, P.A. (1999). *Comparison of factor analyses of handwritten and word-processed writing of middle school students.* Eugene, OR: RCTP.

Hollenbeck, K., Tindal, G., Stieber, S., and Harniss, M. (1999). *Handwritten versus word processed statewide compositions: Do judges rate them differently?* Eugene, OR: University of Oregon, BRT.

Holland, P.W., and Wainer, H. (1993). *Differential item functioning.* Newbury Park, NJ: Erlbaum.

Kopriva, R. (2000). *Ensuring accuracy in testing for English language learners.* Washington, DC: Council of Chief State School Officers.

Kopriva, R.J., and Lowrey, K. (1994). *Investigation of language sensitive modifications in a pilot study of CLAS, the California Learning Assessment System* (Technical Report). Sacramento, CA: California Department of Education, California Learning Assessment System Unit.

Koretz, D. (1997). *The assessment of students with disabilities in Kentucky* (CSE Technical Report 431). Los Angeles: University of California, Los Angeles, National Center for Research on Evaluation, Standards, and Student Testing.

Koretz, D., and Hamilton, L. (1999). *Assessing students with disabilities in Kentucky: The effects of accommodations, format, and subject* (CSE Technical Report 498). Los Angeles: University of California, Los Angeles, National Center for Research on Evaluation, Standards, and Student Testing.

Koretz, D., and Hamilton, L. (2000). Assessment of students with disabilities in Kentucky: Inclusion, student performance, and validity. *Educational Evaluation and Policy Analysis, 22*(3), 255-272.

Lord, F. M. (1980). *Applications of item response theory to practical testing problems.* Hillsdale, NJ: Erlbaum.

Malouf, D. (2001). *Discussion and Synthesis.* Paper prepared for Workshop on Reporting Test Results for Accommodated Test Examinees: Policy Measurement and Score Use Considerations, November 28, Washington, DC.

Marquart, A., and Elliott, S.N. (2000). *Extra time as an accommodation.* Madison, WI: University of Wisconsin.

Mazzeo, J., Carlson, J.E., Voelkl, K.E., and Lutkus, A.D. (2000). *Increasing the participation of special needs students in NAEP: A report on 1996 NAEP research activities.* Available: <http://nces.ed.gov/nationsreportcard/pubs>. [May 17, 2002].

McKevitt, B.C., and Elliott, S.N. (2001). The effects and consequences of using testing accommodations on a standardized reading test. Madison, WI: University of Wisconsin.

National Assessment Governing Board. (2001, May). *Report of the joint meeting of reporting and dissemination committee and committee on standards, design, and methodology.* Washington, DC: Author.

National Center for Education Statistics. (2000). *Becoming a more inclusive NAEP.* Available: <http://nces.ed.gov/nationsreportcard/pubs>. [May 17, 2002].

National Institute of Statistical Sciences. (2000). NAEP inclusion strategies: The report of a workshop at the National Institute of Statistical Sciences, July 10-12.

National Research Council. (1997). *Educating one and all: Students with disabilities and standards-based reform. Committee on Goals 2000 and the Inclusion of Students with Disabilities,* L.M. McDonnell, M.J. McLaughlin, and P. Morison (Eds.). Washington DC: National Academy Press.

National Research Council. (1999). *Grading the nation's report card.* Committee on the Evaluation of National and State Assessments of Educational Progress, J.W. Pellegrino, L.R. Jones, and K.J. Mitchell (Eds.). Washington DC: National Academy Press.

National Research Council. (2000). *Testing English-language learners in U.S. schools.* Committee on Educational Excellence and Testing Equity, K. Hakuta and A. Beatty (Eds.). Washington DC: National Academy Press.

National Research Council. (2001). *NAEP reporting practices: Investigating district level and market-basket reporting.* Committee on NAEP Reporting Practices, P.J. DeVito and J.A. Koenig, (Eds.). Washington DC: National Academy Press.

Olson, J.F., and Goldstein, A.A. (1997). *The inclusion of students with disabilities and limited English proficiency students in large-scale assessments: A summary of recent progress* (NCES 97-482). Washington, DC: National Center for Education Statistics.

Pedhazur, E. (1997). *Multiple regression in behavioral research* (3rd ed.). New York: Harcourt Brace.

Phillips, S.E. (1994). High-stakes testing accommodations: Validity versus disabled rights. *Applied Measurement in Education, 7,* 93-120.

Plutchik, R. (1974). *Foundation of experimental research* (2nd ed.). New York: Harper & Row.

Rivera, C., and Stansfield, C.W. (2001, April). *The effects of linguistic simplification of science test items on performance of limited English proficient and monolingual English-speaking students.* Paper presented at the annual meeting of the American Educational Research Association, Seattle, WA.

Rivera, C., Stansfield, C.W., Scialdone, L., and Sharkey, M. (2000). *An analysis of state policies for the inclusion and accommodation of English language learners in state assessment programs during 1998-1999.* Arlington, VA: George Washington University Center for Equity and Excellence in Education.

Shepard, L., Taylor, G., and Betebenner, D. (1998). *Inclusion of limited-English-proficient students in Rhode Island's grade 4 mathematics performance assessment.* Los Angeles:

University of California, Center for the Study of Evaluation/National Center for Research on Evaluation, Standards, and Student Testing.

Schulte, A.A., Elliott, S.N., and Kratochwill, T.R. (2000). Effects of testing accommodations on standardized mathematics test scores: An experimental analysis of the performances of students with and without disabilities. Madison, WI: University of Wisconsin.

Sireci, S.G. (1997). Problems and issues in linking assessments across languages. *Educational Measurement: Issues and Practices, 16*(1), 12-19.

Taylor, W. (2002). *Analysis of provisions of ESEA relating to assessment.* Paper prepared for March 22 meeting of the Board on Testing and Assessment, Washington DC.

Thompson, S.J., and Thurlow, M.L. (2001). *2001 State special education outcomes: A report on state activities at the end of the century.* Minneapolis, MN: University of Minnesota, National Center on Education Outcomes.

Thurlow, M.L. (2001a). *State policies on accommodations and reporting: Overview of results from surveys of state directors of special education.* Paper prepared for workshop on Reporting Test Results for Accommodated Examinees: Policy, Measurement, and Score Use Considerations, November 28, Washington DC.

Thurlow, M.L. (2001b). *The effects of a simplified-English dictionary accommodation for LEP students who are not literate in their first language.* Paper presented at the annual meeting of the American Educational Research Association, April, Seattle, WA.

Tindal, G., Anderson, L., Helwig, R., Miller, S., and Glasgow, A. (1999). *Accommodating students with learning disabilities on math tests using language simplification.* Eugene, OR: RCTP.

Tindal, G., Heath, B., Hollenbeck, K., Almond, P., and Harniss, M. (1998). Accommodating students with disabilities on large-scale tests: An experimental study. *Exceptional Children, 64*(IV), 439-450.

Trimble, S. (2001). *Kentucky's policy and reporting results for accomodated test takers.* Paper prepared for workshop on Reporting Test Results for Accommodated Examinees: Policy, Measurement, and Score Use Considerations, November 28, Washington DC.

U.S. Department of Education. (1994). *The NAEP 1992 technical report* (NCES Report No. 23-TR20). E.G. Johnson and J.E. Carlson (Eds.). Washington, DC: Author, National Center for Education Statistics.

U.S. Department of Education. (1999). *The NAEP guide* (NCES Report No. 2000-456). N. Horkay (Ed.). Washington, DC: Author, National Center for Education Statistics.

Appendix
A

Workshop Agenda

The National Academies
Board on Testing and Assessment (BOTA)

Reporting Test Results for Accommodated Examinees:
Policy, Measurement, and Score Use Considerations
Green Building, Room 104, 2001 Wisconsin Ave., NW
Wednesday, November 28, 2001

8:00   Continental Breakfast

8:30   **Welcome and Introductions**
- Lauress Wise, Committee Chair and BOTA member
- Patty Morison, Associate Director, Center for Education, National Academies

PANEL 1: POLICY AND LEGAL CONTEXT

Objectives: Lay out the policy context for the workshop and frame the major issues to be addressed.

Moderator: Lorraine McDonnell, University of California, Santa Barbara

Policies and Plans for Reporting NAEP Results for Accommodated Examinees
Peggy Carr, National Center for Education Statistics
Jim Carlson, National Assessment Governing Board

Legal Reasons for Providing Accommodations
Arthur Coleman, Nixon Peabody LLP

Potential Future Uses of NAEP
Thomas Toch, Brookings Institute

10:00   Break

10:15   PANEL 2: STATE POLICIES ON ACCOMMODATIONS AND REPORTING

Objectives: Learn about state and local experiences with respect to: (a) translating accommodation guidelines into practice; (b) making reporting decisions for accommodated test takers; and (c) using results for accommodated individuals. Identify lessons learned that can be of assistance to NAEP's sponsors.

Moderator: Charlene Rivera, Center for Equity and Excellence in Education, George Washington University, Washington DC

Overview: Results from Surveys of State Directors of Special Education
Martha Thurlow, National Center on Educational Outcomes, University of Minnesota

Preliminary Findings: State Policies for the Inclusion and Accommodation of English-Language Learners for 2000-2001
Laura Golden and Lynne Sacks, Center for Equity and Excellence in Education, George Washington University, Washington DC

Kentucky's Policies on Reporting Results for Accommodated Test Takers
Scott Trimble, Director of Assessment for Kentucky

Texas' Policies on Reporting Results for Accommodated Test Takers
Phyllis Stolp, Director of Development and Administration, Student Assessment Programs, TX (by phone)

12:00   Lunch

12:45   PANEL 3: THE EFFECTS OF ACCOMMODATIONS ON TEST
         PERFORMANCE: RESEARCH FINDINGS

         Objective: Learn about the results of empirical research on the
         effects of accommodation on performance on NAEP and other
         assessments.

         Moderator: Margaret McLaughlin, University of Maryland,
         College Park

         **Report on 1996 NAEP Research Activities on
         Accommodations**
         John Mazzeo, Educational Testing Service

         **Testing Accommodations: Legal and Technical Issues
         Challenging Educators (or "Good" Test Scores Are Hard to
         Come By)**
         Stephen Elliott, University of Wisconsin

         **Universally Designed Accommodations for High Stakes,
         Large-Scale Assessment**
         Gerald Tindal, University of Oregon

         **Effects of Accommodations on Test Performance: Research
         Findings for English-Language Learners**
         Jamal Abedi, University of California, Los Angeles, and Center
         for Research on Evaluation, Standards, and Student Testing
         (by phone)

         Assessing Students with Disabilities in Kentucky
         Laura Hamilton, RAND Corporation, CA (by phone)

2:45   Break

3:00   PANEL 4: DISCUSSANTS

        Moderator: Lauress Wise, Human Resources Research
        Organization, VA

- Eugene Johnson, American Institutes for Research, Washington DC
- David Malouf, Office of Special Education Programs, U.S. Department of Education, Washington DC
- Richard Durán, University of California, Santa Barbara
- Margaret Goertz, Consortium for Policy Research in Education, University of Pennsylvania

4:30   **Group Discussion**

5:00   Adjourn

Appendix
B

Workshop Participants

Jamal Abedi, University of California, Los Angeles
Jim Carlson, National Assessment Governing Board
Peggy Carr, National Center for Education Statistics
Arthur Coleman, Nixon Peabody LLP, Washington, DC
Richard Durán, University of California, Santa Barbara
Stephen Elliott, University of Wisconsin
Margaret Goertz, Consortium for Policy Research in Education
Laura Golden, Center for Equity and Excellence in Education, George
     Washington University
Laura Hamilton, RAND Corporation, Santa Monica, California
Eugene Johnson, American Institutes for Research
David Malouf, Office of Special Education Programs, U.S. Department
     of Education
John Mazzeo, Educational Testing Service
Patty McAllister, Education Testing Service
Gary Phillips, National Center for Education Statistics
Lynne Sacks, Center for Equity and Excellence in Education, George
     Washington University
Phyllis Stolp, Texas Office of Assessment
William Taylor, Attorney at Law, Washington, DC
Martha Thurlow, National Center on Educational Outcomes, University
     of Minnesota

Gerald Tindal, University of Oregon
Thomas Toch, Brookings Institutes
Scott Trimble, Kentucky Office of Assessment